IS IT ADD?
A Home Evaluation Guidebook

Isaac N. Silberman, M.D.
&
Arthur Asa Berger, Ph.D.

Writers Club Press
San Jose New York Lincoln Shanghai

IS IT ADD?
A Home Evaluation Guidebook

Published by Writers Club Press
an imprint of iUniverse.com, Inc.

For information address:
iUniverse.com, Inc.
620 North 48th Street
Suite 201
Lincoln, NE 68504-3467
www.iuniverse.com

ISBN: 0-595-09546-1

Printed in the United States of America

Preface

(How You Can Deal Effectively with Your Child's Learning Disabilities and Behavior Disorders and Identify Frequently Overlooked Treatable Medical Problems)

Many children with a behavior problem or ADD diagnosis really have other problems that are primary. These 26-Questions provide a screening tool to select out those who are at high risk for **frequently overlooked medically treatable problems** affecting the brain. There is a subgroup of those with medically treatable brain dysfunction who are significant increased risk for anti-social behavior. **Also—many with "learning disabilities" can be helped more. Without medical treatment the psychosocial stresses precipitate a large number of this subgroup into anti-social and criminal behavior. With medical treatment—even in the presence of psychosocial stress, this subgroup has a much lower incidence of criminal behavior.** These statements are based upon the examination of hundreds of children and thousands of adults.

We should try and use this simple screening tool with many more school, residential and juvenile justice groups of children. We are very interested in your feedback. Comments, suggestions and inquiries can be sent to:

Isaac N. Silberman, M.D.
2000 Van Ness Avenue
San Francisco, CA 94109
FAX (415) 383-5430
E-mail to ins@hooked.net.

Acknowledgements

Many people have helped with discussion and ideas which directly and indirectly have helped develop this book as well as the ideas which will be seen in the Appendix: Arthur J. Mischeaux, P.A., Carolyn Brown, Ph.D., Andi Jobe, PB.S.-M.A., Robert Sinaiko, M.D., Michael Lerner, Ph.D., John Collins Foundation, The Bothin Foundation, Commonweal, Neil Scheiman, Miki Shimi, O.M.D., Mark Steinberg, Ph.D. and Joanne M. LeDuc.

Contents

Chapter 1

How This Book Will Help You: Empowering Parents and Teachers

This book is designed to empower parents and teachers. It is designed to help you avoid wasting money on inappropriate and ineffective treatments for your children, from five to fifteen years old, with learning disabilities and behavior disorders.

You Don't Have to Be Left Out

Too often, parents and teachers find themselves left out of the decision making when it comes to dealing with children with learning disabilities and behavior disorders. They recognize that a child has problems but after that, various experts take over and parents lose control over what is happening. This leads to many calamities.

It is estimated that 85 to 95 percent of the time, the correct diagnosis of medical problems is based on getting an adequate case history and using the information contained in it. Too often, because of time pressures or the particular interests of those who are called in to help (physicians, psychologists, and others), an adequate medical case history is not made, and starting off without the right information, experts go astray.

This simple, easy to follow, guidebook helps you get essential information about your child's problems and helps you figure out what to do. It provides a practical, cost-effective way for you (parents and teachers) to determine whether medical evaluation and treatment is necessary, and if so, suggests what kinds of treatment to consider.

A Bio/Psycho/Social Approach

IS IT ADD? A HOME EVALUATION GUIDEBOOK will help you avoid expensive, unneeded and often counter-productive treatments by psychologists, psychiatrists, neurologists and other kinds of health professionals. Quite often experts tell us, "we won't know whether this course of treatment is working unless it is tried for six months." In some cases, this advice is correct; you can't always expect immediate results. But in many cases, it is not…because experts have, so to speak, "blinders" on to everything except their particular notion of how to proceed.

This book takes a biological, psychological and social approach to treating learning disabilities and behavioral disorders. Sometimes, physical ailments are at the root of a child's behavioral problem, and bio-feedback or psychotherapy is ineffective, whereas drugs are very effective. In some cases, problems children face in their day-to-day lives, and their relations with their siblings and parents, lead to learning disabilities or behavioral problems. Unlike many other books, this book deals with all three of these matters:

A.   your child's physical body and biological processes,
B.   your child's mental states, and
C.   your child's experiences in society.

Chapter 2

A Note on the 26 Key Questions

We have developed 26 key questions which you and your child can answer "yes" or "no." These help identify often overlooked medical problems which can be helped. Case histories will illustrate many details. The 26 key questions are listed below.

PARENTS: THIS FORM TO BE COMPLETED **FIRST** WITH CHILD

NAME:_____

DATE:_____

EVALUATING YOUR CHILD: 26 KEY QUESTIONS

1. At times are you unable to pay attention for more than 3 to 5 minutes?   !Yes   !No

2.   Do you space out? Do people tell you that   !Yes   !No
      sometimes you have a blank look or pale
      look on your face?

3.   Do you daydream? Do people tell you that   !Yes   !No
      you have a staring expression on your face?

4.   Do you get upset when things you have   !Yes   !No
      organized get messed up?

5.   Do you ever feel suspicious of others (paranoid) !Yes   !No
      for no reason?

6.   Do you ever do the same things over and over,   !Yes   !No
      with or without being aware of
      what you are doing?

7.   Do you become suddenly angry for no reason?   !Yes   !No

8.   Have you been getting into   !Yes   !No
      physical fights or yelling fights?

9.   Do you have problems in any of these: !Yes   !No
      reading, writing, math (arithmetic),
      reversing numbers or letters or
      lining numbers up in lines for addition?

10.   Do you ever become confused when   !Yes   !No
      you are trying to think?

11.   Even when you are paying attention,   !Yes   !No
      do you ever have trouble understanding
      what is going on?

12. Do you have a hard time remembering things   !Yes   !No
     that have happened to you or things
     people have said to you?

13. Do you have poor ability to make friends or   !Yes   !No
     are you fearful of making friends?

14. Do you ever have ideas that keep   !Yes   !No
     going through your head?

15. Do you fantasize or think about unreal things   !Yes   !No
     a lot of the time? Can you tell the difference
     between what is real and what is unreal?

16. Do you often feel very   !Yes   !No
     depressed (sad, cry, no energy) or have you
     ever been told you look depressed by others?

17. Do you feel sick or allergic after   !Yes   !No
     breathing certain things, eating certain foods,
     or taking certain medicines?

18. Do you have, or have you been told that   !Yes   !No
     you have, rapid and unreasonable changes
     in your behavior?

19. Do you have times when you have very high   !Yes   !No
     energy (compared to your usual energy level)?
     Or do you have times when you
     have **very** low energy (compared to your usual energy level)?

20. Do you have frequent ear or throat infections?   !Yes   !No

21. Do you have frequent skin irritations or rashes?   !Yes   !No

22. Do you have difficulty with your sense of smell?   !Yes   !No
     Do you ever lose your sense of smell?

23. Do you have problems with seeing or   !Yes   !No
     suffer from double vision?

24. Do you have a hearing problem?   !Yes   !No

25. Do you have any problems with   !Yes   !No
     your sense of taste?

26. Are you very sensitive to pain or touch?   !Yes   !No
     Do you have any other unusual responses to
     pain or touch?

Ask your child to answer these 26 questions. "YES" answers very often indicate an <u>OVERLOOKED MEDICAL PROBLEM</u>, which can be helped. The medical problem (or problems) frequently require a <u>COMBINATION</u> of treatments. These are education, diet, medication and other treatments.

Chapter 3

The Story of James: Or $10,000 Down the Drain

James' parents came to me after having wasted $10,000 on diagnoses that were incorrect and treatments that were ineffective. He'd had years of psychotherapy and tried biofeedback, and nothing worked. His parents tried these approaches because he had lapses of attention. At times, he'd go into a room to get something and return with something else. He also complained that at times he didn't understand what people were saying to him and also he learned things and then promptly forgot them.

The school psychologist examined James and concluded that James had Attention Deficit Disorder. Generally people with Attention Deficit Disorder have attention lapses, poor impulse control and a number are hyperactive. But James was a nice, friendly kid, who was not hyperactive and didn't have a problem with impulse control. James was eleven years old when I first saw him.

When he was eight, his pediatrician thought James might have some kind a problem with his nervous system, and sent him to a neurologist, who gave him an electroencephalogram (EEG) and said that James was normal. As a result of this finding, his parents and doctors thought he had no physical problem and that his difficulties must be psychological. But years of therapy and biofeedback didn't help James. A six month trial of Ritalin (a stimulant) had caused a slight improvement in his attention but he continued to have the significant difficulties with his memory as well as difficulties with understanding things. That's when his parents came to see me.

I had mailed them a questionnaire with 26 key questions that I've developed over the years as a means of identifying selected problems people have. (These questions will be listed and explained in detail in the next chapter. Also, I sent a more elaborate set of follow-up central nervous system questions and a history form for getting a detailed case history. These forms are provided in Appendices A, B and C.) His family brought these questionnaires to the office consultation. The answers indicated the likelihood of a neurological problem that could be helped with medication. Then I spent a considerable amount of time talking with James and his parents, getting additional detailed history of his problems and finding out about his activities. This was followed by a neurological examination.

I gave James an EEG and decided that it was not normal, and that it indicated some subtle problems with the way his nervous system functioned. (I think the EEG was mildly abnormal—some doctors, I should point out, would interpret the EEG as at the far end of the curve of normalcy. There is, of course, a certain amount of judgment involved in reading EEGs, but we have fairly precise information of what is normal and abnormal.) His EEG had an excess of periodic slow activity that was more prominent in the left temporal region. That means that were some possibly abnormal discharges of electrical activity that can be associated with brief disturbances in thinking and memory. This type of slowing is, in many situations, regarded as within the wide range of normal-for-the-age. However, because of the information I gained from his case history, I decided James' EEG probably reflected an abnormality. The brain has a continuous development (that is reflected in changes in a person's EEG) from before we are born until about the age of twenty-six or twenty-eight.

As a result of getting a detailed case history and of my EEG test, I decided that certain medications were worth trying. I prescribed Tegretol (an anti-convulsant medication—which stabilizes the brainwave activity) and in two weeks his parents noted an improvement in James. In addition to prescribing the Tegretol I discussed with both James' parents and James what his problem was and how we were going to approach his treatment. I indicated that the problems were not James' fault and certainly not his parents' fault. I also indicated to them that some of the educational material that I was giving the parents should also be provided to his teachers.

In addition, I volunteered to talk with his teachers on the phone and did arrange for a conference with his primary teacher and school principal. I emphasized to James as well as his parents that it was desirable that he and his parents meet for several times over the next year with a school counselor to assist James and his parents to understand and work out some of the problems that were present secondary to the delays in some parts of his education. With the dramatic improvement I continued to emphasize the need for some on-going psychological counseling and supplemental assistance with his educational program over the year that followed. James continued to do well and since then has successfully completed high school and entered college and is enjoying sports, school and getting along well socially.

In some cases, it is necessary to modify medications that are given; it's not always possible to figure out what medication is best or will work. Often, in addition to giving medications, others things have to be dealt with: your child's diet and your child's social life. Frequently, children with undiagnosed neurological problems are thought to be manipulative or troublesome and people react to them in negative ways—which compounds the problem.

Had the physicians who treated James earlier done a suitably detailed case history and asked enough appropriate questions about the possible physical bases of his memory losses and learning difficulties, it is quite likely that James' parents would have avoided the heartache caused by his not improving, and the expense of his treatments cost. They would have saved more than $10,000 wasted on useless and inappropriate treatments. But what are you to say when an expert, with the authority of a medical degree or doctorate in psychology, tells you, "I think we should try psychotherapy" or "I think biofeedback might help."

Here is a summary of the additional information gathered to provide you a view about how certain clusters of symptoms and findings led to the diagnosis in James' situation. He answered the 26 key questions as indicated on the copy of his answer page that follows. In reviewing the history and the 26 questions at the office he did indicate problems with reversing numbers and letters at times while writing (Question 9). Also he indicated that he would have allergies that were seasonal (hay fever) and with certain foods—milk and chocolate (Question 17). Milk and chocolate seemed to cause stomachaches **at times**. Upon further inquiry he **reported stomach aches** without allergies and **without milk or chocolate**—for no known reason. His **parents** then, when asked, **indicated that he** sometimes seemed to have more difficulty hearing or understanding when he had stomach aches. Also at times **when** he had **stomach aches** they seemed to think he would have **more problems paying attention** to his task or to what they said (Questions 1 and 24). It turned out that they indicated on the extended general medical history that for several years he had special education for an "auditory processing" problem. This auditory processing problem was inconsistent—meaning sometimes his hearing and processing seemed to be normal but at other times was abnormal and his speech therapist and teachers did not understand why he should have erratic responses. Also note that at age 2-6 he had treatment for recurrent ear and throat infections. These infections had been brought under control with treatment by a pediatrician and an allergist and at this time were not thought to be a concern.

The family history was significant in several respects. His father and older brother are both professionals, hardworking and the only known health problem relates to seasonal allergies. His mother's health is reported as good but she indicated she felt somewhat dominated by her husband and this had brought up a host of questions about psychological issues. She also was being given some blame for not properly setting limits for James.

What we see here is a cluster of "yes" answers as reflected with "yes" answers for Questions 1, 2, 11, 12, 17 and 24. (See James' completed 26-Key Question questionnaire.) The element that relates all of these is that they are episodic—short-lived symptoms which occur without apparent reason and then with total recovery to a better state of function. This type of cluster is diagnostic of a temporary disturbance in brain function. Usually it is due to a primary abnormality in the brain's electrical activity. This occasionally can be additionally triggered by such internal factors as: metabolic problems, for example, dietary, diabetic, etc., or with external factors as: stress, shortage of oxygen, inhaling allergens or irritants to which they are sensitive, e.g., gasoline fumes. Note that Question 9, which is about (among other things) reversing numbers and letters are only episodic in connection with a number of other factors noticed like spacing out and problems with hearing. Also note that the episodic quality of the stomachaches and hearing problems point away from a structural problem, i.e., damage to the nerve of the ear or something like a bowel obstruction or specific food allergy.

The associated report of past history of ear infections and allergies is important in that a number of children with various attention problems and learning disabilities have these associated problems which need to be dealt with but at the same time frequently so overshadow other parts of the history that the other positive answers, as in James' situation, are not even explored. Also note that the information elicited in the general history about his mother's being dominated by James' father and her being blamed (which she indicated when I talked with her separately) was one more element which permitted the examining professionals to get diverted from some of the principle problems. One additional lesson to be learned from James' history is the need to ask people what other observations or symptoms—particularly among the 26 key questions—or otherwise, come together in a cluster.

The answers James gave to the 26 key questions follow.

PARENTS: THIS FORM TO BE COMPLETED **FIRST** WITH CHILD

NAME: James _____

DATE: 4/12/89 _____

EVALUATING YOUR CHILD: 26 KEY QUESTIONS

1. At times are you unable to pay attention for more than 3 to 5 minutes? ☒Yes   !No

2. Do you space out? Do people tell you that sometimes you have a blank look or pale look on your face? ☒Yes   !No

3. Do you daydream? Do people tell you that you have a staring expression on your face? !Yes   ☒No

4. Do you get upset when things you have organized get messed up? !Yes   ☒No

5. Do you ever feel suspicious of others (paranoid) for no reason? !Yes   ☒No

6. Do you ever do the same things over and over,   !Yes   ☒No
    with or without being aware of
    what you are doing?

7. Do you become suddenly angry for no reason?   !Yes   ☒No

8. Have you been getting into   !Yes   ☒No
    physical fights or yelling fights?

9. Do you have problems in any of these: ☒Yes   !No
    reading, writing, math (arithmetic),
    reversing numbers or letters or
    lining numbers up in lines for addition?

10. Do you ever become confused when   !Yes   ☒No
    you are trying to think?

11. Even when you are paying attention,   ☒Yes   !No
    do you ever have trouble understanding
    what is going on?

12. Do you have a hard time remembering things   ☒Yes   !No
    that have happened to you or things
    people have said to you?

13. Do you have poor ability to make friends or   !Yes   ☒No
    are you fearful of making friends?

14. Do you ever have ideas that keep   !Yes   ☒No
    going through your head?

15.   Do you fantasize or think about unreal things   !Yes   ⊠No
      a lot of the time? Can you tell the difference
      between what is real and what is unreal?

16.   Do you often feel very   ⊠Yes   !No
      depressed (sad, cry, no energy) or have you
      ever been told you look depressed by others?

17.   Do you feel sick or allergic after   !Yes   ⊠No
      breathing certain things, eating certain foods,
      or taking certain medicines?

18.   Do you have, or have you been told that   !Yes   ⊠No
      you have, rapid and unreasonable changes
      in your behavior?

19.   Do you have times when you have very high   !Yes   ⊠No
      energy (compared to your usual energy level)?
      Or do you have times when you have very
      low energy (compared to your usual energy level)?

20.   Do you have frequent ear or throat infections?   ⊠Yes   !No

21.   Do you have frequent skin irritations or rashes? !Yes   ⊠No

22.   Do you have difficulty with your sense of smell? !Yes   ⊠No
      Do you ever lose your sense of smell?

23.   Do you have problems with seeing or   !Yes   ⊠No
      suffer from double vision?

24.   Do you have a hearing problem?   ⊠Yes   !No

25. Do you have any problems with   !Yes   ☒No
     your sense of taste?

26. Are you very sensitive to pain or touch?   !Yes   ☒No
     Do you have any other unusual responses to
     pain or touch?

Ask your child to answer these 26 questions. "YES" answers very often indicate an <u>OVERLOOKED MEDICAL PROBLEM</u>, which can be helped. The medical problem (or problems) frequently require a <u>COMBINATION</u> of treatments. These are education, diet, medication and other treatments.

Other case histories in this workbook will give you additional insight in how to gather and associate meaningful information. This book will provide you with ammunition; it will help shift the power from the experts and place it back in your hands and in your child's teacher's hands. Most of the problems children face with learning disabilities and behavior disorders become apparent when they go to school and have to interact with other children and have to function in a structured environment, where their ability to learn is an important matter.

WHAT THIS HOME EVALUATION GUIDEBOOK DOES

This book does the following things:

1. It provides a simple, inexpensive way for you and your child's teachers to determine, earlier than other methods do, whether a medical problem, which in many cases could be helped easily, is present.
2. It helps determine whether a medical problem exists by offering a list of 26 key questions that indicate whether or not there is a likelihood of a medical problem and if so, what kind of help should be sought.

3. It has an Appendix with a number of features: follow-up questions to help in interpreting the original 26 key questions.

Forty-Four Years of Experience Counts for Something

This book is based on more than forty years of my practice as a neurologist. I believe that patients should be empowered and that parents and teachers of children with learning disabilities and behavioral problems should—and must—play a bigger role in the treatment of their children. If you have a child with learning disabilities or behavioral disorders, this book will help you see these problems in a better light and gain an understanding of ways these problems can be treated that you might not have considered before.

Since I am a neurologist and psychiatrist, who deals with disturbances of the nervous system, a large number of children that I see have physical (biochemical, hormonal, metabolic, and so on) components to their behavior and learning problems. Many of these children have symptoms whose causes are not obvious and are frequently overlooked. These symptoms frequently can be better treated when their physical cause is recognized and treated. Too often there is exclusive focus on the psychological, educational, and social part of the treatment.

This group constitutes a much larger percentage of children with ADD and ADHD and other learning and behavior problems than is generally recognized. That is, in a significant number of children with these problems, there is an organic (physical) component. Because of the nature of the problems they have, these children require a disproportionate amount of attention and resources. These resources would be more effectively used if better diagnoses were made and integrated with the school programs of these children.

Chapter 4

Evaluating Your Child : 26 Key Questions, with Case Studies

Answering these 26 questions will provide you with important information about your child. This information will be the basis of your decision-making and will help you determine whether your child needs medical attention, and if so, what kind is probably most appropriate. It is important, then, that you answer each question as completely and honestly as you can.

The focus of these questions is to help parents, teachers and physicians sort out those children who have medical problems that frequently aren't recognized but that need to be evaluated and treated with physical and medical means. **In most cases**, of course, **educational, psychological and social interventions are also needed.**

In this chapter, we will discuss each of the 26 questions that are at the heart of this book. We will explain what we mean by each question, sometimes in considerable detail. It is impossible to cover every possibility, of course, but we will provide enough explanation to guide you. We will also offer case histories, examples that will help you understand what each question means and enable you to answer it as accurately as possible.

This bio-psycho-social approach enables parents and teachers to avoid going off on the wrong track and to avoid wasting money on inappropriate and ineffective treatments. **If your child is not making good progress or is continuing to have difficulties, you should go over these questions with him or with her and answer them as accurately and honestly as you can.** And then, on the basis of the answers, you will have a guide to help you better participate in decisions with your health care provider.

After we discuss the questions, you can fill in the questionnaire with your child. It is unlikely that your child will have difficulties with everything on the list, but often you will find that you will be answer yes to a number of the questions.

As an introduction, let us point out that in many cases, health professionals and other so-called "experts" neglect the fact that many symptoms and behaviors have a physical component. That's why these questions are important. They will help you identify when there is a physical component and help you obtain the right kind of assistance.

> ### 1.   At times are you unable to pay attention for more than three to five minutes?

The attention span of children varies a great deal. It is not unusual for children to have occasional periods when their attention spans are limited, but it is unusual for a child from five to ten to consistently be bothered by short attention spans. If children are interested in something, like a television program, they can concentrate on it for a substantial period of time.

If your child has problems concentrating on anything for more than a few minutes, that probably reflects a physical problem—but almost certainly it is not solely caused by Attention Deficit Disorder. Attention, of course, is a very complex and ambiguous concept, so it is a tricky thing to determine whether a child does have problems that are properly identified as Attention Deficit Disorder.

In the United States, five to ten percent of school aged children are considered to have an Attention Deficit Disorder. Twenty percent of the K-12 children are thought to have significant learning disabilities—many times confused with Attention Deficit Disorder. In Great Britain, on the other hand, only two percent of school aged children are thought to have this problem. It is quite likely, then, in the United States we are mistaking other problems for this disorder. And this tendency to over diagnose or misdiagnose often leads to incorrect evaluations of children and treatment programs for them.

It is impossible to isolate any of these questions, since they always occur in clusters, but we can provide an example that will give you a good idea of what we are talking about in this question, when we ask whether your child cannot, at times, and with a certain degree of regularity, pay attention to something for more than three to five minutes.

CASE HISTORY: RALPH

Ralph was, and is, a very bright young child. He seemed to need very little sleep, even as an infant, and before he was three years old he recognized letters and words and learned poems easily. When he started at school, at age five, however, he was an increasing problem to his teachers. He always was interrupting class by blurting out answers, teasing the girls next to him, and fidgeting in his chair.

At age six, he was increasingly driving his mother crazy because he was asking questions about everything and not listening to many of her answers. At school, on the playground, he wouldn't obey the rules and suffered a broken wrist and various other playground accidents more often than most other children. In class, even though he understood things, he seemed to have increasing difficulty with learning to sit and write or focus on reading for more than a couple of minutes.

We're talking about a matter of degree here. It isn't unusual for children, at times, to be unable to concentrate or fidget, but when a child behaves like Ralph, clearly something is wrong. By age seven, the teachers were criticizing him for not cooperating and his parents were frustrated by his being bright but earning D's and F's in his courses. He was getting depressed by all the criticism directed his way. At this time, he decreased his eating and was not gaining weight at the expected rate. His pediatrician identified his problem as being thyroid hyperactivity and also a diagnosis of Attention Deficit Disorder with Hyperactivity.

Ralph's parents had, in the meantime, taken him to a therapist, who suggested that Ralph was not eating because he was suffering from depression. The efforts used treating Ralph for his thyroid problem, Attention Deficit Disorder with Hyperactivity, and therapy helped marginally. The pediatrician had also added Ritalin to the treatment program. It was at this point after six months of treatment with combinations noted and having limited success that I first saw Ralph for evaluation and treatment recommendations. Administering the twenty-six questions identified the issue of significant food and pollen allergies. I then gave him some additional allergy/food questionnaires that identified further detail. This information was relayed to his pediatrician who, in collaboration with me, placed Ralph on a treatment program with certain limited dietary restrictions as well as desensitization for the pollen allergies. With this additional treatment he started eating normally and within three months became much calmer and stopped provoking his teachers and fellow students. He also had a marked improvement in his school work. Ralph's experience is one that illustrates the existence **at the same time** of three problems—all of which must be evaluated and treated to be helpful.

As you have seen in this history about Ralph and as you will see in the other cases frequently there is confusion about what really is and what is appropriately called Attention Deficit Disorder and/or Attention Deficit

Hyperactivity Disorder. There is lots of detail in the formal definitions as provided by a committee on nomenclature representing various specialty groups of physicians in this country and another somewhat different definition is provided by a national group. Here I will just mention two items and then give more details of the "official criteria" that are used by people to consider this diagnosis. In summary, if one has problems with attention and concentration, organization and easy distractibility that first shows itself before age seven and continues for a period of six months it may fall into the category or diagnosis of Attention Deficit Disorder. If these symptoms of attention deficit are also associated with hyperactivity, impulsivity and frequent inappropriate running, climbing and always seem to be driven and these symptoms last for more than six months, this is called Attention Deficit Hyperactivity Disorder—Impulsive Type. I would emphasize that the essence of much of this workbook is to assist you to identify other problems that may mask or incorrectly be included into these two categories or may much less frequently co-exist with a ADD or ADHD.

> **2.   Do you space out? Do people tell you that sometimes you have a blank look or pale look on your face?**

By spacing out, we mean having many times when you are thinking of something, talking with someone, or doing something you are interested in, and you lose track of what has happened. You seem to have forgotten what is going on; it is as if you've suddenly gone to sleep for a few seconds to a minute or two. People may tell you that you have a "blank" look on your face. They may say, for example, "we just talked about that—weren't you listening?" Or you may be talking with someone on the phone and forget who you are talking with or lose track of the subject being discussed for a few seconds or so.

One thing that happens is that people with ADD and ADHD sometimes make mistakes in math or typing that are unusual for them. Watching television they will lose track of the action, even though they understood what was going on and were following it carefully. For an illustration of what we are talking about, let's look at the case history of Alice.

CASE HISTORY: ALICE

Alice, when she was seven, occasionally said she didn't hear her mother when she asked Alice to help with the dishes. Her mother didn't understand this, because Alice liked to help out when she was asked. Then her mother noticed, when she was reading Alice a story she liked, that Alice at times would ask about a line that was just read about a character in the story, saying she had not heard anything about him.

Alice, however, had a good memory and this made no sense to her mother. Sometimes, when skipping rope, Alice would be having a very good rhythm and be singing happily. Then, suddenly, for no apparent reason, she would miss a couple of words in the song she was singing. As these lapses in memory increased, and the number of times when she appeared not to hear others also increased, her mother took her to their pediatrician. Hearing tests were normal, as was the general examination.

Alice seemed, at times, not to be paying attention and was beginning to have difficulties at school, so she was referred to a psychotherapist. The psychologist saw her for play therapy for one year. This seemed to make Alice a little bit more comfortable about things going at home but did not help at all with regard to her schoolwork. One of the reasons why the psychologist and Alice's mother thought this would be a good idea was that Alice's parents were undergoing a divorce and it was thought this was the root of her problems—having this variable attention and then beginning to do poor work at school. After one year, when the divorce process was still going on, Alice's schoolwork was to continue to be getting worse—in spite of the fact that Alice was happy with the psychologist and the therapy seemed to be going okay, except that there were not results with regard to her schoolwork. During the second year of therapy, her mother was asked to come in for a session once a week with Alice and then once a month for the remainder of the year. This again helped Alice understand what was going on with regard to her parents but for reasons that were unclear her schoolwork continued to be a problem and Alice was worried about this. At that point the psychologist had noted on several occasions that Alice did have some blank expression on her face and it turned out that when she discussed this matter with Alice's mother, her mother had also observed some of these blank expressions as well as the fact that Alice's memory seemed to be inconsistent (but at the same time it was "good"). It was inconsistent in the sense that at times she seemed to hear certain things and not remember them, but when she was paying attention, her memory seemed to be better than that of her mother. At that point the psychologist suggested a referral for neurological consultation and the results are noted here.

A neurological consultation and testing with an electroencephalogram (EEG) revealed that Alice's problems were only psychological in part. The main problem was caused by an easily treatable and correctable disturbance in her brain rhythms. The EEG is a safe test (it uses no needles) that records the electrical activity of the brain. Alice had a type of partial seizure that caused her lapses in attention. The concerns she had about her parents' divorce just made things worse and confused her doctors. She was treated with Neurontin (a medicine which stabilized her brain waves). The cause of the problem was explained to Alice, her mother and teachers. She did much better in four weeks and after two months' treatment with Neurontin had symptoms only once a week and then less often over the next year.

Answering these twenty-six questions would have enabled Alice's mother to avoid most of the costly and unnecessary additional testing and psychotherapy that were excessive, as it turns out, in this particular case. True, her parents' divorce was causing Alice some problems but the primary problem here related to an underlying partial seizure disorder causing a lapse of attention which was at the root of her learning problems at school. Once the treatment with medication took place, an occasional visit to the psychologist proved sufficient and as Alice became more comfortable with her improved schoolwork, she was better able to cope with and understand some of the events related to her parents' divorce.

---

3.   Do you daydream? Do people tell you that you have a staring expression on your face?

Many times, when children really don't want to daydream, when they want to concentrate on something of interest, they find themselves daydreaming anyway. That is, they are unable to resist daydreaming and this daydreaming interferes with their doing things they want to do.

Daydreams are lapses in attention in which people muse about things or don't focus on what is going on around them. It is a time when your attention to the world around you and vigilance about this world is decreased. But at the same time, you aren't necessarily having any physical or psychological problems that are causing you to try and avoid the "real world." That is, it is perfectly normal to daydream, and to have reveries, but it is problematic when you daydream at inappropriate times.

When we daydream we can be "reached." If someone calls to us or touches us, they can get our attention. This is in contrast to periods of "spacing out" or when we have periods of staring expressions on our face—during such a time, we cannot be reached. These "spacing out" or staring expressions are caused by a physically based disturbance in brain function.

CASE HISTORY: DIANNE

This very bright and happy child was brought in by her mother on referral from a treating psychologist. When first seen by me she was seven years old. It turns out that at around age three, although she was getting along well, she had some allergies that responded to treatment. Her mother, when asked about whether Dianne had anything unusual about her behavior at age three, said "no." Then, when asked if Dianne would sometimes be very bright and attentive and, at other times, lose track of a conversation, her mother said "yes."

I asked the mother "did Dianne act difficult during those periods when she lost track of a conversation?" The mother said "Oh, no...I didn't pay any attention because she was just daydreaming." This supposed daydreaming and losing track of conversations, along with her inability to follow directions at times, was not regarded by her mother or her pre-school teachers as abnormal. In part, this was because Dianne was so cheerful and bright. She had an IQ test when starting kindergarten, because her mother was involved in education, that confirmed that Dianne's IQ was well above average.

Then, over the next couple of years, at school and at home, the number of times during which her mother and her teachers thought Dianne was daydreaming, increased. Along with this, she began to have more periods of forgetfulness and by third grade was beginning to do poorly in school. Because of this she had a repeat testing by the school psychologist that revealed an unexplained significant drop in her IQ.

At this point, she was having problems with focusing and increasing periods forgetfulness. The diagnosis of Attention Deficit Disorder was made by the school psychologist. Dianne was referred to a private psychologist for further evaluation and treatment. The psychologist did note that the family history included close relatives who suffered from depression and alcohol abuse. Then the psychologist started weekly therapy—psychotherapy and cognitive retraining—with Dianne. The reasoning by the psychologist was that she may have some family basis for what the psychologist described as "unexplained periods of depression and unconscious resistance" to her mother, who wanted Dianne to do much better in school.

This treatment—weekly sessions with Dianne and once-a-month family therapy conferences with both parents and Dianne—continued for six months. At this point, as Dianne continued to do more daydreaming and started doing worse at school, the psychologist referred Dianne for a neurological consultation.

Dianne's case illustrated that frequently, even with very motivated parents and a supportive school system and private resources, one can get into a track of treatment which is not helpful and doesn't address the primary problem. During her examination Dianne was cheerful. Her general physical, neurological and psychiatric examination all appeared normal at first. However, it was evident during the course of the exam that she would occasionally pause when asked something and occasionally have a very brief—lasting perhaps a few seconds—blank appearance.

I asked her mother about this and she said "Oh, that's the way Dianne always daydreams." I had my technician do an EEG on her. This revealed a type of abnormal (paroxysmal) activity that was at the upper limits of normal for a child this age. My reading of her EEG differed with a reading of an earlier EEG done a number of months before by another neurologist. This neurologist had reported Dianne's EEG as normal to her referring pediatrician.

Once her pediatrician was told that Dianne's EEG was normal, the pediatrician decided that Dianne's problem was psychological in nature. On the basis of her case history, and with the additional information provided by giving her a very detailed examination, I came to a somewhat different conclusion about her diagnosis. The fact that her EEG was at the "outer limits" of normal for her age, became very significant, when combined with the other symptoms and problems reported by her parents and teachers.

Let me make an important point here: the relationships in the case history is the engine that drives the decision-making machine.

I obtained additional information (via an extensive case history) that indicated to me that Dianne's EEG is consistent with an abnormal brain wave pattern which is seen in many children who have forms of seizures. (If one did EEGs on a hundred children of Dianne's age, the findings in her EEG would be associated with a high percentage of children who have problems similar to her. If one has a completely normal EEG in children her age, there would be a very low percentage of children with her types of problems.)

I discussed Dianne's problem with Dianne, her mother, the referring psychologist and her teacher. I encouraged continuation of supportive psychotherapy for the mother and infrequent play therapy for Dianne. She was also started on a medication—Depakote (an anti-convulsant/central nervous system stabilizing medication). This medication was given to help stabilize the abnormal electrical activity of her brain. It was this abnormal electrical activity that was associated with and the indication that part of her daydreaming was due to physical causes. The history gave the clues and identifiers that her blank periods were due to a physical cause and the EEG was an additional bit of laboratory evidence here that fit in with the entire picture. The teacher helped all of us monitor her progress. After three months all could see the significant school progress. Dianne's mother also observed the depression and lapses of attention clearing. Of course, this all helped her mother feel better.

I should point out that the psychological factors present in Dianne's case were important, but of secondary significance. These psychological factors should be treated once the physical problem is attended to and beginning to be stabilized. In many situations one has to try and coordinate the parallel treatments of the physical problems, psychotherapy, educational therapy and other needed interventions.

---

4.   Do you get upset when things you have organized get messed up?

Some children like to have their room, desk, books, papers, toys, etc. in a particular organized way. They will, of their own volition, set things in particular places. Other children are not particularly concerned about this. Where there is a problem evident is when a child will organize his or her things in a certain way and then either, an accident or somebody else intentionally changes things. Some children will scream or cry or even attack someone if their things have gotten messed up. This may occur even though the mess-up was an accident.

This type of behavior, especially if it occurs when the child has not been provoked intentionally (by having things messed up), is usually an indication of an emotional problem. If this happens frequently or with small changes, it sometimes represents a serious problem. Even though in popular psychology, this kind of behavior might be considered evidence of an obsessive personality, due to strictly psychological causes, there is evidence now that in many situations there is a neuro-physiological basis for this behavior.

Sometimes there is a family history of obsessive-compulsive behavior. (This behavior is characterized by a tendency to be unrealistically preoccupied with counting or collecting or with having particular thoughts that a child cannot get out of his or her head, and so on.)

Questions 4, 6 and 14 are all designed to get at the matter of obsessive-compulsive traits. Each of these questions assists the interviewer with identifying different ways in which this type of thinking and behavior may be expressed. All of these ideas and behaviors, when they occur infrequently, or in connection with a special project, can be totally normal. It is when they are occurring frequently and are distressing or disruptive to the child or the child's friends and parents, that we should look more carefully and evaluate the significance of this thinking and behavior.

CASE HISTORY: ABIGAIL

Abigail is a twelve year old girl who was diagnosed as having Attention Deficit Disorder and obsessive compulsive disorder. She was referred to me for further treatment. She was also diagnosed as having an eating disorder (at times being unwilling to eat most table foods). Her teachers reported she was easily distracted and had focusing problems.

It was evident from the mother and previous records that Abigail was a brilliant child. Also, she had had three years of therapy with a psychoanalytically oriented therapist, who was being seen weekly. It was troublesome to Abigail as well as to her parents that she couldn't make friends and would frequently become extremely upset about trivial things. At times this was when she could not win a game that she was playing on a computer and at other times when her mother dusted her room and knocked over a container of pencils and pens. Also, there were times when she would spend a week writing a paper and then tear it up, rather than turn it in to her teacher.

Abigail had been given a number of the medications usually used for compulsive behavior, such as Prozac and Tofranil. When first seen by me she was on Anafranil. When I examined her, she was an attractive girl, who was pleasant and cooperative. Her general and neurological examination was normal with the following exceptions: an occasional jerking of her head to one side and what sounded like a nervous cough. Then she would sometimes take a tissue and clear her throat and spit into it.

Laboratory studies, including blood tests and an EEG, revealed no diagnostic abnormalities. The family history was of note in that both parents were professionals—one in the medical field and the other in a scientific field. Both were working. Also, both parents were extremely strict in their demands and expectations of what Abigail should be doing at school and socially. This continually created turmoil when her parents were at home.

Her parents tried to limit her choice of friends, determine her choice of computer games to play, and would not let her go to the local shopping mall alone. These restrictions were reported by both Abigail and her parents to cause an increase in her head-jerking, coughing and spitting.

Abigail also would make up very elaborate and interesting science fiction stories and sometimes read or relate part of these to her mother. This sometimes seemed to provide a way for Abigail and her mother to have a better relationship. However, at times, midway in a story, her mother would say she didn't understand something in the story or would suggest a slight change—this would lead to an explosive reaction at times, with Abigail tearing up the story and telling her mother to leave the room.

When I asked Abigail about what happens when she gets upset with her mother or has these movements of her neck, she explained "I seem to have some buildup of energy and then I can't contain it and it explodes as a neck movement or a cough."

My assessment of the situation was that Abigail had Tourette's Syndrome. This is sometimes associated with a combination of different symptoms and behaviors. For example, Abigail would write compulsively, but when her stories weren't "perfect" in her eyes, she would tear them up in a fit of anger. Her mother's inquiries were viewed as criticism and suggestions that her stories weren't "perfect."

The head and neck movement (tic movement) as well as the cough and effort to cover up with tissue, are a type of movement frequently seen with Tourette's. The restrictive demands made on Abigail by her parents conspicuously increased her symptoms. It is of note that both of her parents had some of these same problems in their childhoods.

Both parents continued to be perfectionists and excessively demanding of themselves in their work and personal activities, but had developed enough ways to compensate for this behavior so that it did not interfere with their daily activities. However, even now, although her parents were successful in work and did enjoy much of their life, they frequently were dissatisfied about their accomplishments. Nothing seemed to be able to satisfy them.

I recommended the following treatment for Abigail.

1. I confronted the parents with the need to be less restrictive. Until I did this, their previous medical contacts had been reticent about dealing with the problem directly. They were able to partially accept and act on this recommendation.

2. I encouraged continuation of the psychotherapy—as there was such a supportive relationship established and at this time Abigail had no other good or close relationships. I indicated to Abigail's parents that in time—when she could establish a relationship with a couple of friends (and perhaps with an adult who was interested in her and her hobbies)—she could gradually decrease her dependence on her therapist.

3. I continued her on the Anafranil.

4. I started her on Klonopin (a medication that helps decrease tics and explosive behavior, as well as being helpful, sometimes, for obsessive compulsive behavior).

After a few months, she had a modest improvement with respect to her tics as well as her relationships with her parents. She also had begun to establish a friendship with one girl at school.

In the course of a couple of years, she made significant improvement with a number of her problems, but continued to have the same difficulties, but the symptoms were less frequent and severe. She also was able to decrease her psychotherapy sessions to once a month and decrease her total medication intake.

Someone with problems similar to Abigail's frequently will need some lifelong follow-up and treatment but can get along well with an integrated program. This involves adjustments over time of medication, proper selection of career and activities, and at times short-term psychotherapy.

> ## 5.   Do you ever feel suspicious of others (paranoid) for no reason?

This type of concern or feeling can, of course, occur because of strictly social or psychological reasons. For example, if you are in a school setting and feel that the other students have nicer clothes than you or are smarter than you, or you are a member of a small cultural minority in some school, you might feel uncomfortable or unduly suspicious, at times, of your classmates. This feeling can be normal and maybe assisted with better communication with a child's classmates or teachers.

Also, a small number of people will have this type of problem due to an inherited tendency to behave in excessively suspicious manner. At its extreme this might show up as a so-called paranoid reaction. This paranoid reaction is an inappropriate feeling and/or attitude towards people or one's environment, a feeling people have that they are threatened or being unreasonably treated. The causes of this can be due to different things, including: unusual allergic reactions to food or pollens; unusual reaction to certain drugs; exposure to certain other toxic agents (such as accidentally ingested poisons found in pesticides or cleaners, or solvents which may be inhaled or absorbed through the skin inadvertently). A small number of people will have a family history of excessive paranoid behavior (sometimes associated with a family history of schizophrenia).

Schizophrenia has a wide number of possible disturbances in thinking, feeling, and behavior. These include inappropriate mood, inability to have a social awareness or relate to others in a meaningful way, extreme ambivalence (inability to make decisions), immature or regressed type of behavior and sometimes hearing voices and feeling unusual powers within oneself or that some outside forces are directing one's behavior, and other expressions of inappropriate behavior.

This type of behavior in many contexts can also be an expression of physical disturbances of the brain function that can be assisted dramatically with certain medications. Some causes of this kind of behavior are head injury, schizo-affective disorders (a combination of schizophrenic and bi-polar illness), some drugs and infections. A type of partial seizure sometimes expresses itself in paranoid behavior. This is frequently not recognized as a seizure because there are no evident abnormal movements or behavior that people usually think of as associated with seizures.

CASE HISTORY: NANCY

Nancy is a thirteen year old girl who at times becomes suddenly angry without reason, and when the does this, also becomes paranoid. She has a history of problems with attention and gets poor grades at school, though her parents and teachers know that she is very bright. She has driven friends, parents and teachers "crazy."

When first seen she had the "baggage" of multiple diagnoses and treatments. These included having been hospitalized, shortly before I saw her, for three weeks at a psychiatric hospital for suicide threats and "management" problems, but she never had a neurological consultation or an EEG. The medication she was on, when I first saw her, was Paxil (an anti-depressant) and Tegretol. She was still having a lot of problems with attention, and it was thought that she was suffering from ADD. She also was very suspicious of her schoolmates, parents, and teachers.

Nancy complained that three medicines she had been taking, prior to her hospitalization, had caused big problems. These were: Zoloft (an anti-depressant), which made her feel nauseous and agitated and caused to her to lose weight; Lithium (a medicine used for bi-polar/manic-depressive illness) which, she claimed, caused her to go crazy; and Ritalin, which she said also caused her to become violent and unreasonable.

When she came to see me, she had heavy makeup on, pierced ears with three earrings in one ear, and looked like a street walker. Her parents, very frustrated by a number of years of unsuccessful treatment efforts, were hostile to me and gave the impression that I—representing the medical community—was responsible for their daughter and their problems and let me know that I was supposed to fix them promptly. They both were professionals who worked and were very busy.

One of Nancy's parents had significant periods of depression which were currently being helped by anti-depressant medication. Nancy's brother also had some symptoms similar to hers, but he was less combative—but also doing poorly in high school. Nancy also had a number of food allergies, which were associated with her being very picky about her eating. In addition, she did indicate that she was very obsessive-compulsive about repeating certain activities like washing her hands or cleaning her room or reorganizing her clothes repeatedly, without apparent reason.

My physical and neurological examination first revealed her to be a healthy girl, except for a significantly abnormal EEG. Nancy was quiet, insightful, and a little bit manipulative and sarcastic. Her reflexes, vision, hearing, coordination, etc. were all normal, but this didn't mean that there wasn't a physical dysfunction with her nervous system. She was also beginning to menstruate and it became evident that her mood swings were more extreme before her menstrual periods. I discussed this with her and recommended some simple treatment options to lessen the impact of her menstrual periods on her mood swings (a low salt diet, taking 50 milligrams of Vitamin B-6, twice a day for five days before she had her periods and during her periods).

She immediately wanted to control and cut the examination short by saying that her mother had to take her home right away to be sure that some house repairs would be taken care of. Her mother, however, informed me that someone was at their home and would be able to take care of things. Nancy then angrily agreed to remain at my office and continue with the consultation.

Communication and follow-up appointments with Nancy and her parents were very difficult for several years. Her parents mistakenly assumed that I and her teachers (and the right medicines) would solve all her problems—without their being actively involved. Over two years time, with difficult negotiations and sometimes unpleasant phone consultations, I was able to get her parents more actively involved, change her medicines and get her into treatment with a psychologist. I also got the school to collaborate more actively in her case.

We stopped her Paxil, and, over the course of a year, increased her Tegretol, added a very low does of Ativan, and had her take Folic Acid (one milligram) to prevent birth defects in the event she became pregnant. I prescribed Ativan (an anti-anxiety medication) to help her break her vicious cycle of anxiety and partial seizures that lead to her become aggressive and paranoid. Nancy's paranoid behavior stopped and her mood swings became much less severe and did not disrupt her school activities.

Her schoolwork also improved. What people labeled ADD, depression and paranoid behavior was, in reality three interacting problems: (1) a type of small seizure that manifested itself in her being easily distracted, having problems in focusing, and having poor impulse control; (2) schizo-affective disorder (a mixture of schizophrenic type symptoms and mood swings); and (3) psychological and social problems compounding these two conditions.

6.   Do you ever do the same things over and over, without being aware of what you are doing?

We all, at times, repeat certain activities. This is perfectly normal. The problem with repeated activities arises when a child will continue to do a certain thing, unnecessarily. For example, a child will wash and dry his hands and then do the same thing again, three or four more times. Another example would be opening and closing a computer program over and over again, to be certain it is closed correctly. In still another example, a child may dribble a basketball endlessly and never take a shot at the basket.

CASE HISTORY: OTTO

When Otto, a ten year old boy, would start playing a board game, or a computer game, he would at first seem to very good at it and then, after a short while, would suddenly stop and have to go back and recheck and question his every move. This seemed to be unnecessary, because he had done everything correctly and "fairly" according to the game rules. Nevertheless, if a friend or his mother would say "you can continue with the game," he would get angry, say he couldn't, and continue to repeat the steps in the game—or throw something.

Otto also had difficulties with inconsistent behavior at school. At times he functioned at an extremely bright level and was able to do work two years ahead of his class. At other times, he seemed unable to do simple things—for example, he would be typing and then, for a few seconds to a minute, he'd be unable to find the letters on the typewriter keyboard. He often would lose his temper and get into fights, which was a real problem.

Another element of concern to his parents was that he had a number of tics (involuntary movements). These tics would show up at times as a very rapid turning of his neck and a compensatory effort to cover this up by putting his hands on his face, as if he were trying to lean on his hand. He would also, at times, have an involuntary movement of his arm and again he would try to make this appear as if it were a natural move or an intentional effort by lifting his arm out in front of himself, as if he were going to reach for something or perhaps scratch his head.

Another feature of his compulsive behavior was that he would describe a story and go on, at extreme lengths, with wild fantasies, which sounded very creative. Then he would lose track of what was fantasy and what was reality.

At other times he would involuntarily make a grunting sound (a tic) that was often connected with chewing and grimacing movements of his mouth. He would try to cover this up by pretending he had a cough and then he would, on his own volition, repeat the cough and mouth movements...to make people think this was some kind of normal phenomenon. Sometimes he exhibited staring behavior.

Another element in his history which was significant was that he had a very high IQ, above 140 (100 is average) and an excellent memory. In addition to all of the above, he had problems falling asleep and exhibited extreme mood swings, going from being very happy to very sad.

Both of Otto's parents were high-powered professionals who worked away from home. He had been undergoing psychotherapy with a psychoanalytically oriented psychiatrist for four years and his psychiatrist had decided not to use any medications with Otto until a couple of months before I saw him.

There were two reasons for this: one, the psychiatrist was very opposed to and uncomfortable with the use of medications for anyone; two, there was a question of this boy being close to losing contact with reality at times (autistic or schizophrenic behavior) and the psychiatrist felt that supportive psychotherapy, without medications, was the best long-term treatment option. The reason for starting medication treatments was that the tics were becoming increasingly disturbing and Otto's ability to even relate in a limited way to his peers at school was being lost.

Several years before he had been given Ritalin for "Attention Deficit Disorder" which seemed to calm him down, but his reaction after it wore off was terrible and could not be tolerated by his parents or friends. Two months before he saw me he was started on Prozac, which did seem to help him with some of his fears—but not his tics or behavioral problems.

Otto had Tourette's Syndrome: some of the classic symptoms and signs associated with it are tics, involuntary verbalizations (grunts, swearing) and obsessive-compulsive behavior. Some people with Tourette's Syndrome also have seizures, manic-depressive (bi-polar) behavior, or both…but these were not diagnosed prior to my consultation. Some of his teachers thought his behavior was the result of ADD—Attention Deficit Disorder—and were pushing to have Ritalin resumed. However, tic symptoms in Tourette's Syndrome are made worse with Ritalin.

At the time when he was first seen he was a good-looking boy who showed no distress. He wasn't concerned about his behavior. He had a lot of evident tics, and gave a very elaborate explanation to explain them (based on chemistry and the laws of physics, which he knew about). He explained that certain energies in his body became focused and then were released by the tics. He was very sophisticated about computers and had designed his own games. The remainder of his examination was normal.

Otto's bloodwork was normal. But his EEG did show an excess of abnormal discharges for a person his age. His EEG could be read as within the wide range of normal for a ten year old—or as borderline abnormal. Otto's EEG could be read as consistent with organic problems (that is, the findings indicate the possibility of physical-electrochemical disturbance but do not prove it). Probably 95 percent of the EEG's of ten year old children would not have this reading. To make a proper diagnosis, one needs to have a reasonable correlation between a patient's clinical history, examination, and laboratory findings (EEG and others). One treats the person not the laboratory test!

Otto was on Anafranil when I first saw him—a medicine useful for depression and for those with obsessive-compulsive thinking that does not respond to psychotherapy or conditioning therapies (biofeedback, etc.) I replaced the Anafranil with Prozac and suggested he continue seeing his psychiatrist, with whom he had a good relationship. After a short time, I gave him Depakote (an anti-convulsant) which is useful, also, for some mood disorders and for seizures.

After several months of Depakote and Prozac, I concluded that the Depakote wasn't helping him and substituted Clonidine. This medication is helpful in reducing tics, obsessive compulsive behavior and bi-polar [manic depressive symptoms]. It sometimes has other benefits. I also suggested he take 50 milligrams of Vitamin B-1, two to three times a day. Overall there was some improvement in his condition over the next few years. He suffered from fewer tics and his compulsive behavior decreased significantly. He was able to get along better at school.

This patient illustrates some of the problems associated with someone who has a number of different problems at the same time. It is important to address the various problems and not get sidetracked with just one of them. It can be argued that many of symptoms and problems that Otto had—and the different diagnostic "labels" given them—are really different expressions of an underlying imbalance of his brain chemistry (neuro-transmitters, neuro-receptors) and other influencing factors such as hormones. We know that a person's total health—in part as expressed by their metabolism—affects the brain and behavior. At this time we only have a very limited understanding of many of the complexities involved in this matter

7.   Do you become suddenly angry for no reason?

When we say suddenly we mean instantly, seemingly out of the blue, without any observable cause. By anger, we mean behavior such as screaming, hitting, and throwing things—especially when this is unusual for the person and seems out of character.

"No reason" is a difficult topic to discuss. Everyone has periods of anger, but when these occur without reason (and in conjunction with one or several of the other questions in the list being answered positively) then we have to be suspicious that this isn't a "normal" childhood behavior.

CASE HISTORY: SALLY

An eight year old girl, Sally, was usually warm and friendly and nice. She was playing with a close friend and suddenly became angry…because she said her friend Matilda took her doll and put it in the wrong place on her bed. Matilda said she didn't touch the doll. Then Sally screamed that her friend was a liar. The girl's mother came down when she heard the two girls yelling and screaming at each other. Sally was screaming and Matilda was crying.

The mother tried talking with her daughter, who seemed totally unreasonable, and said "I never want to see Matilda again. I wish she would die." Sally had hit her friend. Sally looked wild and when her mother tried to comfort her, Sally started hitting her mother, also.

The mother talked with Sally's teacher as there had been questions of why Sally was having more trouble with learning to read as well as transposing letters and numbers when she was learning to write. Actually this had been noted when Sally was in the first grade but as there was a family history of some learning disabilities and dyslexia, it was decided to see if she would do better with regular classes and without special attention. This decision was agreed on by Sally's teacher and mother as Sally was very good with music, athletics and social skills. It was thought that emphasizing her learning disability with special tutoring would cause Sally to be more insecure and self conscious.

The teacher also commented that when Sally was six and seven, there was a possibility that she had an Attention Deficit Disorder—as she would seem to be very inconsistent in her ability to focus and also seemed to be forgetful of things that she had learned. When the fight occurred and then the mother discussed this with Sally's teacher, a reevaluation was decided upon.

For this little girl and her friend to have such a fight seemed extremely unusual. Also, Sally's teacher reported that Sally had been in several fights in recent months. In addition, the teacher asked Sally's mother about Sally's being so sad for several weeks at a time during the past semester. The key here is that Sally had episodic changes in her usual mood and behavior which is a red flag alerting us to the fact that her behavior is something to be concerned about.

After seeing a school psychologist she was referred to me. I found Sally to be a bright, cheerful child who had four problems identified on the questionnaire and this was followed with an EEG that was distinctly abnormal for a child of her age. Her history revealed a family history of reading difficulties, bi-polar (manic depressive) illness, and seizure disorder (complex partial seizures). In addition, her parents had marital problems, which were currently very severe.

Sally's getting angry without apparent reason was due to her getting a little upset because she had reading problems which were exacerbated by her inability to concentrate, due to her seizure disorder. Also, at times she was unable to understand what her girlfriend had said (because Sally was in the midst of a small seizure where her comprehension was interfered with) and this caused misunderstandings, which led to fights. Her "blanks in attention" which were thought to be ADD actually turned out to be a learning disability complicated by partial seizures. Complicating all of this, Sally had periods of depression due to an inherited tendency to mood swings.

Sally's physical examination was normal. That is, all of her general examination, except for the neurological examination, was normal. She had a subtle but definite abnormality in her reading and writing of some words and numbers, which was an indication of her having a physical disturbance of her brain. Two points should be made here:

First, frequently a school learning disabilities specialist will identify problems like Sally's in a child. However, they are frequently approached as strictly an educational issue.

Second, when children like Sally are referred to psychiatrists and/or neurologists, they will frequently report that the child's neurological examination is normal. This is because the physicians often do not get as detailed a medical history as is needed and usually will not order an EEG.

I discussed my findings with Sally's mother, Sally, and her teachers. Then I started her on Tegretol (a medication which helps stabilize brain wave activity, mood swings and anger outbursts). I also recommended that Sally have counseling and some special education assistance. Her parents were also encouraged to seek some assistance for their marital problems. Over the next two years, Sally did much better in her schoolwork and her relations with others. Please refer to Question 9 for additional findings that are sometimes associated with learning disabilities and related problems.

8.	Have you been getting into an unusual number of physical fights or yelling fights?

Children often get into fights with one another, but it is unusual for a child to get into many fights in a given day...and to continue getting into fights with regularity. The unusual feature of these fights is that at times a child will get into fights with a close friend for no apparent reason. Also, afterwards a child may say "I don't know why I got in a fight" or "I don't remember being in that fight." This same child can have a usual loving personality and getting in and out of fights seems to be totally out of character. There are other behavioral patterns associated with this problem that will be discussed in the case history below.

It is obvious that many of the behaviors discussed in these questions overlap. Thus, you will notice that in this question we are again discussing fighting—but here we are interested in verbal aggression rather than physical aggression. That is, we are interested in yelling fights rather than physical fights. The two, of course, often occur at the same time.

By yelling fights we mean a time when, without a reasonable cause, a child will start screaming. This screaming is often in response to a question about what the child is doing or some very casual inquiry where the child was at some period of time.

CASE HISTORY: CASS

Cass is a thirteen year old boy. One day he said that when he was at school, some boys in his class claimed that he had drugs in his locker. They then reported him to the teacher, who asked him whether it was true or not. Cass denied it. The teacher said that two classmates had reported him. Cass first yelled at the teacher, who subsequently contacted his mother. When Cass came home, he was confronted by his mother about the report of his having drugs in his locker. At first he claimed he didn't hear what she said. When his mother repeated herself, Cass started screaming at his mother, saying he had been falsely accused.

In another instance, Cass was talking with his mother and was smiling and seemed to be happy and then, when she asked him about some book he was reading, he suddenly got an angry expression on his face and he screamed at her, "mind your own business." After then, he got up and took a pillow and threw it at her. He then sat down and started crying. When his mother asked him what he was crying about, he did not answer. Then, within a couple of minutes, he asked her what she was angry about and seemed to be feeling happy again. These events were particularly upsetting to Cass' parents as he had been a "model" child until about six months before this report of drugs being found in his locker. Cass' parents asked him about whether he had been using drugs and he denied it. He also again got very angry that they implied they did not believe him.

Cass' parents were very strict and a number of disciplinary measures were immediately instituted. This included not being able to go out with his friends in the evenings or weekends for a couple of weeks. This led to more arguments between Cass and his parents as well as more problems with his teacher at school. The parents were asked to meet with a school counselor and Cass to discuss things and once a week counseling was started for one month. At this point things were continuing to get worse. Cass, because of his multiple problems, had a number of labels thrown at him. I will just mention a few of these to try and alert you to the fact that these labels frequently **misrepresent** what is going on. These labels cause some therapists to feel they understand a particular problem. What is really going on is that **the diagnostic label permits the therapist to have a conscious or unconscious explanation/excuse why the child is not making progress.** Things like conduct disorder, oppositional behavior, passive-aggressive personality, oppositional-defiant disorder and other labels are thrown together to "identify the character of the problem." In the Appendix I will give a little bit more of the official "criteria" for these various categories and try and help alert you to the idea that labels do not explain by themselves what the problem is, what the cause of it is or what the best treatment approach should be. One must try and get at the cause of the problem, understand it and then treat the cause in the best coordinated way possible.

What we see here is a combination of the appearance of a changing personality and mood changes which were at first attributed to street drug use. Other possible explanations including communication problems between the teacher, the students who reported him, and his parents were considered—but the decision was made that they were probably not the cause of the problems. Also, medical problems like diabetes, subtle nutritional or digestive problems, allergies and environmental toxins, etc., were initially not explored.

He was then taken to his pediatrician who found no clear-cut cause of his problems on routine examinations and routine blood tests and he was then referred to me for evaluation. On taking his history and that of his parents several additional facts emerged. First, his parents were extremely strict and this had been a problem to him increasingly since he was eleven years of age and was restricted more than his peers. Then, at age twelve, he had a bike accident with a brief loss of consciousness and no apparent residual problems. Also, six months before the reported drug problem at school he had had a couple more bouts of tonsillitis and associated ear infection.

When I examined him he seemed to be somewhat irritable and either would not answer my questions or seemed extremely uncomfortable and restless during the examination. He was unable to say anything critical about his parents—even when they were in the waiting room and out of earshot. It certainly appeared that he was unhappy about their attitudes but could not bring himself to say anything to me. His electroencephalogram and was normal and so was his neurological examination. I requested some blood tests. The blood tests gave indication of a possible low-grade residual infection as well as an increase in one part of the cell count that suggested possibly allergy, parasites or some other abnormal reaction.

At this point further discussion with his parents revealed that there had been a very profound change in his personality from being easy-going and calm to irritable, short-tempered and doing more poorly in school in the previous four to five months. I referred him to an allergist/immunologist who made the diagnosis of a residual chronic infection (possibly associated with his previous tonsillitis) and gave him a different course of treatment as well as a special diet. The treatment by the allergist/immunologist involved another course of anti-biotics followed by Nystantin, an anti-fungal agent, and diet to treat a residual fungal infection which had developed over the years. He improved over the next few months but continued to be somewhat irritable and was then referred back to me again.

In reviewing his problem again it appeared that the combination of Cass' mild concussion, then his tonsillitis and residual infection had caused a personality change, which was then precipitated into many other problems he had. His parents' attitude at that point had also changed toward him, and that, combined with his adolescent development, accelerated all the problems. The change in treatment that we then instituted was **supportive therapy** and **counseling for his parents and Cass separately** as well as giving him a little bit more freedom, which his parents did with great reluctance, only after considerable pressure from the therapist. Gradually over the next two years his behavior returned to normal for him and the initial bouts of yelling, mood changes and other problems that followed cleared up.

> **9.** **Do you have any problems with any of these: reading, writing, math (arithmetic), reversing numbers or letters or lining up numbers in line for addition?**

Learning disabilities are frequently associated with a diagnosis of Attention Deficit Disorder and/or Attention Deficit Hyperactivity Disorder. Just a few words about identifying learning disabilities. The most conspicuous manifestations of learning disabilities are learning the basics of reading, writing, math, comprehension, vocabulary and difficulties with arrangements of objects and pictures—all with respect to what is appropriate for the age and cultural group being reviewed.

It is important to keep in mind that children vary in their development. The presence of one component of learning being a problem does not, by definition, mean that there is a major learning disability or that the learning disability, even when there is a problem, is the primary cause of the child's problems. Having said that, we know from many observations as well as many studies done over the last 50 years that **a large percentage of people who have serious problems with the law and wind up in juvenile hall and/or state or federal prisons have significant learning disabilities.**

This is not to say that a child with a learning disability is going to become a criminal. The simple and most likely explanation of this association between learning disabilities and legal and social problems is that there is a predisposition to get into difficulties if one has problems in dealing with society and problems in dealing with day-to-day activities, which, of course, includes the minimal basic information and education that is needed to deal with many job situations. When one adds the learning disability to social and economic issues the odds are increased that there will be more problems in this group of children.

There are too many so-called "tests" for evaluating and using as guides to identifying learning disabilities. At the same time many subtle forms of difficulty with language, things like right/left differentiation problems and other easily identified educational problems are overlooked or not adequately treated until the child becomes older, if they are treated at all. For example, some children are very bright—but seem to have problems with some information they hear. They may seem to ignore or mess up with verbal instructions but do well with reading, writing, math, memory tests and therefore are labeled with various incorrect diagnoses like "oppositional" or "defiant." Their problem might be selective "auditory aphasia", a condition where one has problems with interpreting information that is heard. What we see, however, is that even when there is clear recognition of a learning disability problem in a child whose physical status is reasonably good with respect to the senses—smell, vision, hearing, taste and feeling—that frequently there are some associated problems in these children that are not given adequate attention, or, on many occasions, not identified. Then, if the focus is strictly on remediating the so-called learning disability, this effort frequently is a failure, as the associated problems need to be treated also or the child cannot be effectively helped. Just to emphasize things that have been brought out in connection with cases illustrating some of the other questions—let's summarize here: **First,** there are some good simple screening tests for learning disabilities and some information about this is in the Appendix. **Secondly,** even when learning disability is the diagnosis and special education efforts are made, one must try and give reasonable attention to the following:

Are there some other general medical problems present which can
be helped?

Are there any significant psychological problems that can be worked with?

Are there significant social problems that are impacting what is going on and that can be helped?

Is there a history in the family of some major medical problem or psychiatric problem—for example alcoholism, substance abuse, frequent job changes, multiple social problems?

Are there marked episodic or fluctuating levels of function in the child? That is, can the child at one time do certain academic work and at another time seem to have totally forgotten or be unable to do this for a short period of time or for a couple of hours and then the next day seem to be able to do it again?

CASE HISTORY: KENNY

One child who illustrates some of the problems that we are referring to is Kenny. Kenny was fifteen years old when he was first brought to see me for consultation and treatment recommendations. At that time he was already in a residential treatment center and had been a ward of the court for one year. This had been in conjunction with his being involved with battery as well as a series of events where he had vandalized stores as well as neighbors' property.

Kenny's past history was extremely informative in that he started to exhibit difficult behavior according to his mother by the age of one. He had difficulty sleeping and was also very "busy" and into things more than the average baby. He also had a tendency to cry for three or four hours an evening during his first year of life. He had some problems in eating, which improved over a couple of years, and also had considerable hyperactivity. By age 5 he had calmed down a little bit. The principle information from his mother was that he had an allergy to milk, which was avoided most of the time. I also learned that one of his aunt's and a great-uncle had emotional problems and other unknown neurological problems. His mother was working throughout this period of time. It was also of note that Kenny had frequent upper respiratory infections as well as ear infections that were treated during his first eight years of life. There were reports that in his first grade class, in another state, he was referred to a child study team, because he was "having a learning disability" and suffered, as well, from an "emotional handicap." His parents moved to California when he was nine years of age and was placed in a special class within the general school district. He made some progress there, but because of continued problems he was referred for another assessment and also Individual Educational Program (IEP) meetings were held to review his progress during the fourth, fifth and sixth grades. His case complicated by the fact that part of the mental health program provided by him to the county was halted for a while because the mother had not returned certain paperwork.

It is of note that there were at least five to six years when he is reported to have been in special education programs and a summary of a so-called three year mandated evaluation when he was 13 gave the following reports. He was essentially one year behind in his math, spelling, language and his reading was close to age and grade level. There is a report that although he was bright and liked the attention when he read out loud, he was frequently distracted or disruptive when reading out loud. He liked to create a bit of turmoil in the classroom if he managed to get the attention of the group. He had considerable problems with adult authority and would become explosive or sullen and then perhaps calm later on when discussing things. It was noted that he seemed to have "insight" within several days after an explosive event was discussed with him but at the same time he did not have any ability to follow through or learn from one situation to the next. With his friends-peers he was well-liked and seemed to be very accepted by them.

As far as his general writing, language, arts and spelling there was the comment that he needed additional "remediation" and had particular difficulty with math problems. There were comments about his **strengths and positive attributes** in that he was bright in many ways and had the potential to function at grade level. However he had the problems noted above. The evaluation team indicated that he had the potential to function at grade level and was talented both with regard to athletics as well as being a natural leader and charismatic. School evaluation by the school psychologists indicated the **great need for close communication and coordination between all of the agencies and people involved in his treatment.** This recommendation took place approximately two years before I first saw him. Note that the school psychologist, where he had been prior to placement in the residential treatment center, was emphasizing the frequent problems he had with attention. One year later, when he became a ward of the court, the highlights that were pointed out in his referral to the residential treatment center were: **explosive temper** and **defiant, abusive behavior, problems with expressing his feelings** and also a **need to perform perfectly** or **blow up if he didn't meet his own "perfect standards."**

At my first examination it should be noted that in the preceding year he had been on a medication called Catapress (Clonidine is the brand name) and this did help him to have fewer explosive episodes as well as to improve his attention span. However, it was noted that when his medication, Catapress was reduced from a higher to a lower dose, i.e., three tenths to two tenths milligrams, he would once again become explosive. **Additional history** that came **from his mother at this time was** that when he was in **his early childhood** and occasionally **even now** that **BEFORE he exploded he was observed to get a red face, red ears** and **then if the tense situation developed further** he would **have a clenching of his fists and some movement and shaking of his feet** if he was sitting and **then explode with the physical violence and verbal outbursts.** My examination revealed that he was somewhat hyperactive during the examination but cooperative. He had a yo-yo in his hand that my assistant had given him and he was constantly playing with this even when I was trying to talk with him or start to do a neurological examination.

Other than the restlessness and the evidence of mild learning disability in terms of some word selection he was bright and cooperative and had no other abnormalities on examination. It should be noted that his IQ on a recent intelligence test was listed as 110 with a good testing overall. An electroencephalogram showed some mild abnormalities but this in itself was not diagnostic, although it did reflect some increased cerebral irritability.

My assessment of him was (1) he had a mild learning disability; (2) he had variable attention due to other problems; and (3) autonomic nervous system instability—as manifested by the presentation of the red face, red ears and other features noted. (The autonomic nervous system is the involuntary/unconscious portion of the nervous system which is involved in and controls such functions as skin temperature, hair rising, involuntary bowel and bladder movements, heart rate and many other "unconscious" features of the nervous system.) After I saw him, I spoke with his mother and then indicated to Kenny that I would be in touch with him and his mother after I reviewed all the records and information that I had, and talked with staff at his residential center. I should mention that during the course of the year that he was at the residential center, a time before I had seen him, that they were working very diligently with a behavioral training program as well as the academic program and continuing on the medication noted.

I recommended after reviewing things that he have added to his medication Klonopin, 0.5 mg at bedtime as well as Zantac, 150 mg at bedtime. Zantac was given as he had reports of digestive problems at times as well as the empirical observation that some children with this cluster of symptoms have done better with the addition of an anti-histaminic type medication, which also decreases the autonomic nervous system response that he reported. He was seen over the next couple of years at intervals of every three months and seen on a daily basis by educational staff and people at his residential treatment center who were working with him in a coordinated program.

There were many ups and downs, including problems where he would be disruptive as well as assaultive and at other times be a leader in the group. He also voiced considerable difficulty with self-esteem. One issue that became conspicuously more evident as a problem was his tendency to become very upset if he did not do some task perfectly. Except for math, when he came to the program he was doing fair in his various school activities **when he was able to concentrate**. He would become extremely perturbed with himself when he would not be able to do the math work.

When the issue of the combination of his perfectionist attitudes as well as his occasionally refusing to cooperate in the program became more prominent, I was challenged by the staff, which indicated that I had two months to try and help him "turn around" or otherwise he was going to be going back to juvenile hall and the chances of his getting future treatment that would be helpful were limited. This timing was due to budget problems.

At this point I added Anafranil, with the concurrence of the court and his mother. Anafranil is a medication that is useful for obsessive-compulsive behavior as well as depression. My thinking here was that in addition to a mild difficulty with learning disability and uncontrolled mood, he had a significant problem with anger and violence, which was further being precipitated by his obsessive feelings, and need to unrealistically demand perfection of himself. After the addition of the Anafranil, he started to be much less impulsive, was less demanding of himself and had fewer incidents where he was assaulting peers and threatening the staff. After a month the staff were quite convinced that the combination of Anafranil (in relatively low doses, 25 mg once a day) as well as the Clonidine (in lower doses, 0.1 mg twice a day) and Klonopin (0.5 mg at bedtime) were helping him much more and the staff efforts for behavioral training and other educational efforts were beginning to show positive results. Also he was more focused and had a couple of months when there were no reports of any explosive behavior or assaults.

During all of this time he was also receiving individual therapy, group therapy at the residential treatment center as well as some special tutoring at school and doing better with his sport activities which he enjoyed. This included football and basketball. Over the next six months he did have several explosive periods and part of these seem to coincide with a decrease in his Clonidine which had been reduced gradually over the year from 0.3 mg daily to 0.1 mg daily. Interestingly, that change was precipitated by a particular staff consultant being excessively tense about the use of three medications simultaneously. I should add that generally the fewest medicines that one can use the better. However, occasionally it is necessary to use three medications and sometimes more.

When last seen after two years of follow-up he was ready to be discharged from the residential treatment center and return home. In the three months prior to his scheduled discharge date he was doing a mechanic's assistant job away from the residential treatment center and was continuing to show improvement. This helped his self-esteem.

We can learn about three things from Kenny's story. **One** is the matter of some identified abnormalities since the first year of life. **Secondly**, the learning disability which was a mild problem, however, associated with and aggravated by the perfectionist tendency. And, **thirdly**, the matter of the autonomic instability. These three together led to temporary criminal behavior which, hopefully, has now been turned around...and he will continue to improve. In his situation, like in many others, the outcome in terms of long-term benefits is best achieved with **continuation of a support program** that includes education, job, behavioral training and medications. **Long-term continuity and integration of programs is critical.**

Learning disability and antisocial behavior and the diagnoses of distractibility and attention deficit were diverting and confusing elements. This cluster of symptoms is seen in many children who wind up as criminals.

> **10.   Do you ever become confused when you are trying to think?**

It is natural for children to become confused, occasionally, when they are trying to think about something or do something. The children we are talking about become confused in situations where they are relaxed and sometimes even when they are happy with what is going on. The point is, that this confusion in thinking happens often when they children are not under any stress and there is no reason (so it seems) for them to be confused.

Children are confused, as we interpret the term, when suddenly they become disoriented—that is, they don't know where they are (while in a familiar place). Or they don't understand a simple story that is being read to them or, when they are playing baseball, they have a sudden lack of awareness about what they are supposed to be doing and don't realize, for example, that they are supposed to run from one base to another. All of these are examples occurring in children who ordinarily can do these things with no difficulty or who can understand the situation they are involved in and act as would be expected.

CASE HISTORY: ARNOLD

Arnold, a nine-year old boy, suffered from periods of confusion and an "Attention Deficit Disorder." Arnold had been referred by a psychologist who had been giving him biofeedback, twice a week, for almost a year—with minimal benefit. The psychologist reported that Arnold's concentration improved slightly, even though his other problems continued.

He would **lose his temper** from time to time and **get into fights** with others. Then, he said he didn't remember getting into these fights. Occasionally, he became **confused** and he would got lost while riding his bike. He had a couple of **falls off his bike**, without any head injury, but couldn't remember the falls. At times he reported a **metallic taste in his mouth** for a few seconds, which would then clear. Sometimes he **reported smelling something burning**—and there was nothing around that was burning. Arnold was overweight and seemed at times to be a compulsive eater of sweets. When he ate lots of sweets he had more episodes of confusion.

The family history revealed a low thyroid condition in Arnold's mother and diabetes in his mother's parents. In children who have a family history of thyroid problems or diabetes, or other medical problems such as allergies and asthma, it is imperative that a comprehensive physical examination, with requisite laboratory tests, be made. [Please see the Appendix for outline of general "comprehensive physical exam" and basic laboratory tests.] A physical examination of Arnold revealed that he was a little overweight but otherwise had no evident problems. However, an Electroencephalogram (an EEG in essence is a recording of brain wave electrical activity) showed a borderline abnormality.

Arnold's EEG, we should point out, would have been read as within normal limits by many competent neurologists—in part because the conception of normality is so broad, especially in a maturing child. In this particular case, Arnold's case history, that is the detailed information about **unusual smells** and **tastes, periods of brief confusion**, and **sudden loss of temper**, are **DIAGNOSTIC CLUES** that something physical was causing his problems.

In Arnold's case we decided to utilized a more detailed questionnaire, which revealed a number of other problems with his central nervous system. [This more detailed questionnaire is found in the Appendix.] It is important to remember that in we must look at everything about the child—and not use only one finding or diagnosis to explain everything—even though that diagnosis explains *part* of the problem.

Thus, we examined and considered Arnold's family history, his psychological problems, his physical condition and his social situation. His situation was complicated by the fact that he was living part of the time with his divorced mother and part of the time with his remarried father and step-mother in a "blended family" with a step-brother and step-sister. His mother and father, we should point out, were both interested in helping Arnold. But it was harder to help him because of the problems in living in two households.

It turns out that when Arnold ate ice cream or other sweets, they triggered partial seizure reactions, also known as a type of epilepsy. His seizures were expressed by the rage reactions and confusion and unexplained falls that often characterized his behavior. He needed to avoid **fast acting** carbohydrates (**sugars**) due to the **family history of diabetes**, which **triggered SOME of his seizures.** We see some children with problems in attention which vary and also associated problems of confusion or sometimes unexplained rage reactions that are triggered by sugars. More of these children are seen among people who have a family history of diabetes. One of the important although it is somewhat infrequent causes of problems with attention, confusion, dizziness and other problems is a low convulsive threshold (lowered tendency to have a type of change in the brain metabolism or vulnerability to have a change in the brain metabolism) which triggers a seizure. The way this works is that some people have a hidden brain vulnerability that doesn't reveal itself when they have an EEG. Only in the presence of a drop in blood sugar will the abnormality, that is no of great significance generally speaking, be triggered and cause a series of partial seizure-like symptoms—confusion, altered awareness, dizziness and other symptoms. There are a number of people who have this problem. If one just addresses the question of the testing for blood sugars or just does a routine electroencephalogram the findings will be within normal limits and the proper treatment will not be made because an adequate identification of the problem is not made. The point of all of this is that if somebody is not responding to standard evaluation and treatment, one should look at some of the more subtle things that are hinted at and can be frequently identified by going into a detailed history. The situation we are describing here is sometimes called a reactive hypoglycemia triggering partial seizures.

Arnold also needed medication to alleviate the symptoms caused in part by the abnormal electrical activity pattern of his brain. [A more intensive evaluation of Arnold's condition, including sleep EEGs, week-long EEGs with telemetry, or the use of electrodes would most certainly have demonstrated abnormal electrical activity in Arnold's brain, which most neurologists would identify as significant for a child his age.] To summarize, as Arnold had three issues that need to be attended to we made arrangements for treatment of all three and explained the total picture to his parents and the explanation was: (1) he had a increased cerebral irritability that predisposed him to having a type of seizure. This particular predisposition to seizures was minor but was triggered by fast-acting sugars. The other associated issue which had to be evaluated and worked with and which was treated was the fact that there were some stresses associated with his living with a blended family. Therefore it was necessary to be sure that both his mother and his father's new families were aware of the situation and that both could be helpful to him to coordinate both his diet and medications as well as to have the small amount of supportive psychotherapy that was needed. Actually over the next four years he did very well and the amount of psychotherapy needed was really very little, i.e., a counseling session with his parents two times in the first month and then once every four to eight weeks over the next couple of years proved sufficient to be helpful and he did very well both at home as well as at school. Obviously there were times when it was difficult for him to refrain from eating sweets and this matter was worked on an on-going basis with a dietitian and his parents so that it was not going to become an increased area of arguments. By the time he reached puberty it was of course even more important that he do more to manage his own medication as well as his own diet and this was worked from the first month after I saw so that once could in a very gradual way prepare him to understand and be interested in managing his own care to the extent possible.

One of the most important areas of treatment of children who have any of these problems is to as early as possible to try and turn over control of their health care both psychological and physical to them so that they are more motivated and interested in following through with the needed program.

11.   Even when you are paying attention, do you have trouble understanding what is going on?

When children are able to understand things, whether they be a little slower in learning than "average" or "average" or "very bright," there are times when they trying to understand what is going on but are unable to do so. This occurs in situations in which it is known that they can understand some information that is given to them, or understand what is going on.

This behavior may be viewed by someone else—a teacher or member of the family—as either being uncooperative or being hostile or wishing to control things by manipulating others. This lack of understanding reflects a brief lapse in their capacity to perceive what is said (due to a partial seizure at times) without any movement of their body or other clues to the untrained observer.

In such situations, a parent or teacher might say to the child, "I know you can do that and that you understood me." The child, who is trying to cooperate, becomes upset that he or she truly did not understand or comprehend the message and is unable to think and behave as expected. Then one often gets into a cycle where the teacher or parent may become critical or abusive and the child becomes overly defensive or paranoid.

CASE HISTORY: STANLEY

Stanley was fifteen when I first saw him. He was referred to me by his pediatrician and his clinical psychologist with a diagnosis of Attention Deficit Disorder. He had received by this time, psychotherapy, educational therapy, and a short course of biofeedback in the previous two years. His father and mother accompanied him to the appointment, as did his younger brother, who was six years old. His parents were increasingly concerned that, at times, Stanley seemed to have trouble acting the way he was supposed to.

The thing which troubled his parents a great deal was that sometimes he understood requests and family rules very well and was very cooperative. And then at other times he would just lose his temper and act as if he didn't know anything about these rules. Then a problem arose between him and his parents, because it appeared that he was lying to them and trying to manipulate them. This, then, led to another problem—because his mother was sure, at times, that he wasn't lying or being manipulative but his father thought that he was. This would lead to arguments between the parents.

Sometimes Stanley could do math problems with ease; at other times, he said he couldn't do them and that he never knew how to do them. After he flunked a couple of math tests at school—and math was something he enjoyed—his parents realized that something was wrong with him. They recognized that he actually hadn't been lying to them during those times when he said he didn't remember the house rules or how to do his math problems.

Before I saw him, Stanley had problems with asthma, but this no longer was troublesome. He had also had a period of time when he was not interested in school, but did like math, science and English, and was getting B's and C's. Also in the background was the fact that his mother had remarried and there was a problem of insufficient interest of his birth father, who saw him once or twice a month. At times Stanley got depressed for unknown reasons.

These family problems (and Stanley's **variable interest in school** and occasional depression, as well as his **presumed lying**) made it appear to his parents and his pediatrician that Stanley's difficulties were due to social and psychological problems.

Disturbances in brain function (biochemically and physically caused) can express themselves in hundreds, actually thousands, of different ways. These neurological disturbances, when expressed by behavioral abnormalities, are similar, many times to the behaviors associated with strictly psychological and social causes. Because of this, we many times see people who have a psychological and/or social problem—but in reality this becomes a red herring that diverts our attention from the associated and frequently more basic and significant physical problem they have.

In many cases, it is possible to offer a psychological, social or economic explanation of some child's problem that is correct, but not adequate or relevant to the child's problem. What I mean by this is that an explanation that is theoretically correct but is not the explanation that is appropriate for this particular child. Another situation that arises is that some of the psychological and social problems that are present are stress factors and precipitants of an underlying physical problem. However, unless one first deals with the physical problem, it will not be possible to be effective with psychological and social interventions.

In Stanley's case, because of the difficulties that were described in relation to his birth-father and school problems (lying and being manipulative), counseling was started. This did, over a couple of months, assist him to be more motivated at school and have fewer problems with his parents. However, he continued to have difficulties with understanding things at times.

When seen at the office it should be noted that he continued to take a medicine—antihistaminic—for seasonal allergies. Also, his parents emphasized that when he was working with his hobby, model trains, his attention and understanding seemed to be very good. (This is a frequent experience—and confusing—that somebody who has physical problems can at times overcome them in areas that they are interested in and very intensely involved in. This leads to doctors and families assuming that there is no physical basis for the child's problem.)

His general examination revealed a minimal problem with coordination of fine movements of his fingers; the only other finding was a borderline abnormal EEG for his age. It had what we refer to as excessively high amplitude and sharp activity which occurred intermittently in the left temporal region. This finding is seen in a small percentage of "normals" at this age. As Stanley had three related and significant findings on history and laboratory it appeared likely that part of the attention problem and understanding problem which Stanley exhibited was due to the combined effect of stresses associated with his family and abnormal brain wave discharges. The third thing that was relevant here is the subtle abnormality on his examination in terms of the fine movement coordination problem which in itself is of no great concern but reflected some evidence of physical brain disease. With this combination of three interrelated problems we decided to go ahead and try a medication which would stabilize the electrical activity of his brain.

We decided to try using a medication to stabilize the electrical activity of his brain. After two months, his periods of lack of attention and variable understanding had markedly decreased. And we then encouraged him and his parents to resume an occasional consultation with his psychologist for family therapy. One of the points that we can learn from Stanley's experience is that labels of being manipulative or obstinate or passive-aggressive and many of the other labels which we hear thrown around like conduct disorder and antisocial behavior, negative behavior sometimes in conjunction with attention deficit disorder diagnosis frequently are more the product of a misunderstanding of what is going on and the child's attempt to compensate for the problems rather than being the correct diagnosis.

For additional ideas and information about some problems which occur which alter attention, mood and present in atypical ways sometimes in association with attention deficit and sometimes in association with other learning disabilities please also see the questions and descriptions noted in Questions 2, 3, 7, 8, 10, 11 and 12. Those questions in particular have a component of a physical/chemical disturbance of the brain which is associated with and contributes to altered thinking problems and thinking, behavior and mood which are frequently not adequately evaluated and addressed. I should add that there are many conditions with organic disturbance in brain function or biochemical disturbance in brain function or biochemical and metabolic disturbance elsewhere in the body which reflects itself in a disturbance in thinking and behavior. Problems which are not seizure disorders but problems which nevertheless can be assisted in part by appropriate use of medication in addition to psychological, behavioral and educational measures.

> **12.   Do you have a hard time remembering things that happened to you or thing people have said to you?**

Although this question is somewhat similar to the one above, it is included to help identify related but different problems. Children often have difficulty remembering what others have told them, but the children we are talking about here have this kind of behavior occur often and in a way that is disruptive to their normal activities.

This problem sometimes occurs in children who have "learning disabilities" which, in part, are associated with some observed physical problem, such as difficulty with speech or fine movements of their fingers. When it occurs in that context, the fact that these children have an associated problem with their memory (which can be helped with an additional treatment) is often overlooked. That is because it is overshadowed (by a focusing on the learning disability) in the thinking of the educator or medical professionals involved in the evaluation and treatment recommendations of these children.

The crux of the matter is that doctors, therapists and others frequently become so preoccupied with one conspicuous problem a child has that, mistakenly, they do not pay attention to other areas of evaluation and treatment in that child that should also be considered. **It is important to avoid falling into the habit of selecting one observation or diagnosis to explain everything.**

CASE HISTORY: JACK

Jack is a seven year old boy who was referred to me with the diagnoses of disturbed behavior, memory problems and learning disability. He was brought in by his adoptive parents. Jack also would have difficulty paying attention and carried a diagnosis of Attention Deficit Disorder with hyperactivity. He frequently got into fights, would appear confused, and also appeared angry at times without apparent reason. He was receiving Ritalin when first seen and was on a restricted diet, trying to avoid foods with additives and fast-acting sugars.

As early as three months of age, he had developmental delays and sudden fits of anger. There is a history of his birth mother having multi-drug use during her pregnancy. Also, seizures were reported at Jack's birth. When he was tested, before being seen by me, he was reported as functioning at the kindergarten level—that is, two years below his chronological age.

He also had difficulties identified with fine motor movements. Previous extensive evaluations by physicians in a health center and psychologists and learning specialists in a program for treatment of children with delayed development reported the following: learning disabilities, attention deficit hyperactive disorder and oppositional defiant disorder. He also carried the diagnoses of allergies to sulfa and penicillin (which manifested themselves as hives and anaphylaxis [a shock-like reaction]) and asthma. He was also receiving desensitization (injections by an allergist) for allergies to soaps and pollens. The allergy symptoms in part should up as red eyes, a runny nose and a times the asthma.

On my examination he had normal findings with the following three exceptions: one, he was extremely hyperactive and negative in the examination room; two, when asked to hold his hands over his head, he had an eversion (a rotation outward of the palm of his right hand) as well as a slight downward drift of the same arm; and three, mild difficulty with fine motor movements of his fingers.

Jack's performance in school was extremely poor. This was attributed to his being hyperactive and uncooperative. He would forget things which he seemed to have learned earlier; then he and the teachers would quickly give up. All of their energies had to be focused on preventing him from disturbing other children.

My additional evaluation revealed that he had a variable level of attention—but seemed to be quite bright at times. An EEG showed minimal/borderline abnormalities. These could not be regarded as significant in themselves. My initial treatment was continuation of the treatment for his allergies, continuation of the Ritalin, and the addition of Tegretol. Tegretol was used to see whether it might reduce Jack's unexplained sudden fights and anger episodes.

In a month there was slight improvement, but it was not very impressive. At this point I put pressure on the parents to get some weekly counseling for the child. Like in many situations, both parents were working, and although there was fair after-school care arrangements, there was a limitation of parental involvement. The combination of the **counseling** and the **additional medication** (Tegretol) seemed to lead to a turning point in Jack's behavior, which improved significantly.

A couple of the lessons that we can learn from Jack's experience are these. First, just because someone has disturbed behavior and learning disabilities it does not mean that issues like allergies and family problems have no bearing. Also, the element of diet was brought in here so what we saw is initially there had been prominent emphasis on the treatment of his allergies and additional focus on the attention deficit disorder diagnosis as the basis for the remainder of his problems. The fact that Jack had had a history of seizures at birth and that his birth mother was a multi-drug user also had a tendency to divert people from the question that perhaps Jack had associated physical brain dysfunction (organic brain disease) which in addition to behavioral methods and Ritalin and diet he could be helped with some other medication as Tegretol or Depakote. The point here is the one that we are making repeatedly is that here we saw a **boy** who does have **multiple problems** but that due to the fact that **several** were more **prominent** and currently active i.e., the allergies, asthma and hyperactivity, **some other issues were overlooked**. As noted, he did begin to show significant additional improvement when counseling, Tegretol, Ritalin, treatment of his allergies and behavioral training programs were all integrated together. Over the course of the next three years he continued to show improvement. It is of interest and importance to note that there were several times in the course of this three years where he was improving where due to logistic issues or changing attitudes of some involved staff working with me in his treatment that one component or another of the treatment would fall by the wayside. For example, there were times when the parents would stop with their counseling sessions and the behavioral training figuring that the medication program and his improvements warranted doing this. He at this time would then begin to slip. Another time they were advised that he could discontinue the Tegretol and he seemed to do okay for a few weeks and then had another relapse in terms of disturbed behavior and more combative behavior as well as doing more poorly at school. It took approximately one year before the adoptive and the other parties of the treatment team realized fully the continuing integrated program with the many different facets of treatment was needed to maintain improvement. At this time he continues to improve and we are optimistic that this will continue and as time goes on he will become a self-sufficient and successful adult.

13.   Do you have poor ability to make friends or are you fearful of making friends?

Pre-adolescents and adolescents have many different patterns of making friends. A significant determinant of children's making friends relates to their peers and adult influences at a very young age. There is evidence that genetic (inherited) factors have some influence on whether somebody is going to be very introverted or extroverted, but these traits can be either encouraged or suppressed by one's home, school and community environment. The time to be concerned, of course, is when a child is not making friends or having difficulty making friends or being unhappy about having no friends. The other two questions that become critical are has there been a significant change either in their way of making friends or their choice of friends?

The point of all this is that attention, concentration and many school and behavior problems may be connected to a child's ability to make and keep friends. Therefore, children who have been getting along well and then experience s a significant change in their behavior, or who have been diagnosed as having a learning disability or ADD, require attention. One must investigate their social history (see how well they socialize with others and examine their home environment) and not just rely only on an educational or medical evaluation.

CASE HISTORY: KATRINA

Katrina was a fifteen year old girl who was referred to me for evaluation and treatment of problems she had with poor attention and memory, depression, headaches, school work and also difficulty in making new friends.

The family had moved from a farm one year before and, as a consequence, she had to start at a new school. Before the move, she had lots of friends, was happy, and was doing well at school.

At first, her family and pediatrician thought that all of her difficulties were due to the move. Also, as she was too far away from an old boyfriend to continue their relationship, this was thought to be another explanation for all of her symptoms. A learning disability evaluation done at her school revealed some subtle problems in memory and written expression—but these did not seem to fit into any usual pattern. It was thought that, perhaps, she was suffering from depression. The family, on advice of school psychologists, had arranged for her to have some counseling, but this did not prove helpful. Katrina's pediatrician concluded, after examining her—because of the combination of her learning disabilities and headaches that Katrina needed a consultation with a neurologist.

I discovered two things when I examined her. She did have distinct problems with cognitive functions (memory, attention, variable ability to do the same task, writing) and a distinctly abnormal EEG for her age. A much more detailed exploration of her history revealed several critical issues. One, in the weeks before she had moved, a neighboring farmer had sprayed a potent insecticide on his field. At that time, she had felt a little bit nauseated, was tired and had a decreased appetite for several days, and experienced tearing in her eyes and had an unexplained skin rash. It turned out that her mother and sister had similar but less severe symptoms.

Then, at the new school, in addition to her not doing well academically, she had trouble making friends and being accepted by her classmates. The classmates, for the main part, had wealthier and better educated parents, and, in essence, were ostracizing her—with a couple of exceptions. In addition, she was unable to participate in the soccer and cheerleading activities that she excelled at when she was at her previous school. This was because her present school required students to pay fees for soccer club equipment and purchase special uniforms—both of which were beyond her family's means. This compounded her problems at a particularly difficult stage in her development (adolescence).

With the above history I ordered additional special blood tests to identify possible residues of toxins in her blood. Some traces of toxic residua were found. My diagnosis for Katrina was as follows. First, she was suffering brain damage from the insecticide spray (technically, residua of toxic encephalopathy). Second, she was depressed. This was compounded by her difficulties with thinking as well as the feeling of rejection by her new classmates. She had additional problems with her self-esteem because she now had difficulties doing well at school (previously she had been an excellent student and this was an area she prided herself in and enjoyed). After obtaining this information from Katrina I talked more with her parents and in essence they confirmed the history that Katrina had given. It also turned out that Katrina's mother and a younger brother and sister had developed symptoms in the previous year but their symptoms were not as profound and their evaluation was still in process with the pediatrician. The probable cause of their symptoms was similar to that of Katrina's.

At this point what I did with the parents was the following: (1) we explained the probable cause of her problem; (2) I asked her to see a toxicologist who recommended a couple of more blood and urine tests to try and clarify further the extent that any residual toxic elements in Katrina at that time.

Regarding treatment a physician who specialized in toxicology and dietetics made some recommendations which primarily focused on diet alterations and supplemental vitamins and minerals. Additional treatment for Katrina included supportive counseling sessions once every two to three weeks as was possible with the logistic issues being dealt and also after several months adding in a medication for her depression. In addition we arranged to have her join the community center in an area a little distant from where she was living where she could feel at home with her peers and this was to assist her to resume developing friends of her own age group. After a year of work with this and for a period of six months supplemental medication to help out with both her depression and to a lesser extent her attention she was making gradual but definite improvement and this has continued over a three year period. We should note that in situations where somebody has a problem with both making friends as well as with a problem with the toxic exposure patience and tincture of time are frequently rewarded as long as one can be persistent. One other comment about the subject of exposures to toxic agents of a subtle variety. This is an increasingly important subject in our U.S. environment and as time goes on we are learning more about it although the subject is still in its early stages of understanding both what is best done for evaluation and treatment of people who have these problems.

> ## 14.   Do you ever have ideas that keep going through your head?

Everyone, at times, has an "internal dialogue." This term refers to the process of discussing things, so to speak, with ourselves. A process like this is normal and occurs regularly. However, in some cases a person reaches the point where he or she gets the equivalent of cracked record a particular idea or conversation continues in their thinking, even though they would like to turn it off.

One example that occurs in a number of children is what they would like to tell their mother or father, who have restricted them for some reason. Thus, a child might think "you're mean to not let me go to the mall after school and I would like to kill you." This thought, at first, starts in reaction to "normal" rule setting by parents and then become a pre-occupation.

In a number of adolescents, this internal dialogue is set in motion when their father restricts their use of the family car. The adolescent then continues to have repeated thoughts about what he or she would like to say to the father. "I feel like taking your car and wrecking it, since you won't let me drive it. I hate you." This is all that the adolescent can think of, and he cannot get it out of his mind. Adolescents feel they can't express such thoughts out loud to their parents, since it would lead to their being punished by even more restriction of car use.

Another example is a child who is constantly afraid that he or she will flunk a test, even though he or she has done very well in previous tests in the same subject. These children worry about tests before they take them, while they take them, and afterwards—to a point that they are very anxious and upset about this matter and can't get the internal dialogue they have about their tests out of their heads. These ideas that keep running though children's heads can be irritating, if they occur once in a while, but can be the cause of great suffering or even disability if they are constant or very frequent.

CASE HISTORY: ROGER

Roger is an eleven year old boy who was referred to me by his pediatrician and psychologist for additional evaluation and treatment of several long-standing problems. He had disturbing compulsive behavior at school—at times he would keep rewriting and correcting an assignment, even though it was well done.

He would also have difficulty shifting from one activity to another, and although he was very bright, sometimes he would use incorrect words or occasionally incorrect sentences (either grammatically incorrect sentences or nonsense sentences). A minute later, when the teacher asked him what he was saying, he could express himself correctly. Also, at times he would, for no logical reason, keep repeating some word over and over again. He would explain this when asked by saying he had this idea and word "going around in his head." And that's why he said it. "He had to."

Roger had a problem from age four to seven of an occasional loss of bowel control (encopresis). He had had extensive diagnostic evaluations by a gastroenterologist (a specialist in stomach and bowel problems). These evaluations had shown no physical cause for Roger's problem. From seven until I first saw him, the encopresis had been controlled most of the time with the use of mineral oil and a regulated diet. At times of stress and when he had some upper respiratory infection, he would have an occasional bowel accident.

The encopresis was thought to be primarily of a psychological nature. He also had periods of being depressed for hours to days, which had no clear explanation or cause. At school he would frequently disturb his class by taunting or teasing other children. At home, he got into many violent fights with his brother, who was two years older.

His parents were very intelligent (both were college graduates). His father had a high position in a large corporation, which required long hours and frequent weekend work at the office. **His mother** was a home-maker who had obsessive compulsive traits and was seeing a psychiatrist and taking medication that assisted her in taking care of her home and other children, who were in good health. **She was OVERLY occupied with scheduled activities** for her children and herself.

In the previous two years before I saw him, his schoolwork had been of poor quality, even though he was intelligent and detailed psychological test-ing had indicated that he should have been able to handle more of the work at a superior level. The psychological testing did reveal some significant but subtle learning disability problems in addition to the obsessive compulsive traits. Roger had problems with writing in a grammatically correct manner and was inconsistent in the way he dealt with mathematical concepts. With time pressures, these difficulties were aggravated.

His treatment in the previous two years had included special educational assistance at school as well as psychotherapy and biofeedback training by a competent psychologist. This had helped a little with regard to his ability to focus, but the problems with repetitive word use and his other problems noted above had not been helped.

When I examined him, he was a good looking boy who was of average height and weight and appeared to be quite healthy. The striking thing about him, initially, was that he was blinking his eyes rapidly, fiddling with a small computer game that he had brought with him, and occa-sionally turning his head and neck to the right. Within a couple of min-utes—when he felt more comfortable with me—he got up and started picking up instruments off my desk, asking what they were for, going behind the examining room chair, looking out the window, and continu-ously asking questions—hearing part of the answer and shifting to another series of questions. It was a little difficult but possible to interrupt him and ask him a couple of questions.

The other thing I noticed was that Roger would respond tangentially at times to an inquiry that he seemed to understand. Also, he would at times seem to have a delay in his response to my questions. I asked his parents about this and they said—"Oh, he always does this. He thinks about the answer." I suspected, on the other hand, that these delays, at times, were due to an interruption in his brain wave electrical activity and other times, were truly due to his pondering the question and the several possible answers that might have come to his mind.

This is an important point. One should try and make additional observations, and ask additional questions, to find out whether these lags in response time—supposedly due to indecisiveness or daydreaming—are the cause of these delays or whether they are due to a type of partial seizure. There are other things that cause delays aside from partial seizures, such as fatigue, poor diet, fear and depression. With partial seizures one frequently gets a history of associated symptoms, such as dizziness, nausea, numbness, tingling of an arm and numerous other symptoms. One might also observe a blank/staring appearance of the eyes or some momentary change in color of the face or some body movements.

I ordered blood studies, an EKG (electrocardiogram), and an EEG. The blood studies and EKG were normal. I interpreted Roger's EEG as borderline abnormal, though other neurologists read it as normal.

I started him on Prozac, to help out with his obsessive compulsive behavior, and also on Klonipin (clonazepam), a medication which is often helpful for involuntary movements and abnormal electrical activity of the brain. He also continued with his special educational programs at school. After a month, as he was only making a small amount of improvement, I discontinued the Klonipin and substituted Depakote.

He did make modest improvement over the next few months and then had a return of some of his symptoms when he got an upper respiratory infection. This was coincident with his father having to work even longer hours at his job and it appeared that Roger's symptoms became worse when his father was unable to spend much time with him. Over the next six months, Roger made a modest amount of additional improvement, but it was evident that he needed individual psychotherapy. His parents agreed and he started in with weekly sessions with an experienced psychiatrist. Over the next year Roger made additional improvements. Small adjustments were made in his medications and increasing collaboration between the school, parents, psychiatrist and myself also contributed to his making more progress.

Over the next couple of years, I adjusted his medications. The psychiatrist decreased the frequencies of visits with Roger to one every four to six weeks and talked more with his mother to alleviate her anxieties. The mother also was receiving more individual psychotherapy from another therapist which proved helpful for Roger, also. After the first year of treatment by his experienced psychiatrist as well as the supplemental support that his mother was able to receive from both their own therapist as well as talking briefly with the psychiatrist before or after he saw Roger improvement became more conspicuous. Roger was more at ease school, his schoolwork improved, the problem he had with disturbing and recurring thoughts was much less prominent. Also, something new developed in that he was able to make a couple of friends at school and have a little bit more interest in other people as well as computers and things which did not require interaction with people. The responses that he gave when one talked with him became more prompt as he could at this time not feel it is necessary to mull over a question multiple times to give the "perfect" answer. Also and interestingly the problems that he had with his encopresis markedly decreased in part due to the fact that he was able to eat a more appropriate diet and be less "picky" about his food and the diet changes themselves were helpful. We have now followed him for five years and he continues to improve and be more comfortable with school, social activities and gets along much better with his brother also and quite critical is the fact that he no longer is teased by children at school and in the rare instance when that does happen he knows how to cope with it in a more natural way.

Important to learn from his story is the fact that his father was more integrated into treatment even though it was phone consultations with the psychiatrist in school which were more regular and the total treatment program was more integrated. Also, one component of his treatment which is important to underline is that although there was a more integrated and effective treatment the frequency and length of medical contacts as such was decreased. This is important in that there are some people particularly those with obsessive-compulsive traits who get into a situation where so much of their time is involved in medical appointments that this just adds to their total burden and compounds rather than proves helpful to their problem.

> **15.   Do you think or fantasize about unreal things a lot of the time? Can you tell the difference between what is real and what is unreal?**

The amount of fantasizing, thinking about imaginary things and having a problem in telling—differentiating—between what is real and what is unreal of course depends on the age and circumstances. Until the age of three certainly and sometimes a little older there are natural developmental phenomena which are associated with a child not being able know what is real and unreal. A problem develops, however, if that continues. Also, if one has an active imagination and thinks about science fiction or fantasy that certainly can be totally within normal limits. Once again, the problem is that this is a preoccupation to the extent that it excludes certain basic needs that the individual has taking care of themselves as far as food, clothing, shelter and dealing with their day-to-day projects. Excess focus on fantasy and inappropriate feelings can have many causes. They can be triggered at times by such things as social and psychological problems. For example, if you are in a school setting and feel that the other students have nicer clothes than you or are smarter than you, or if you are a member of a small cultural minority in some school, you might feel uncomfortable, suspicious and then in turn try and escape into fantasy and at times develop an unduly suspicious attitude. Certainly at times some of this attitude of trying to escape the reality and be unduly suspicious can be a natural defense mechanism and not in any way a reflection of a problem. It may be assisted by better communication between the child's classmates and teachers.

Also, a small number of people have this type of problem of being unreasonably suspicious and having problems sometimes associated with difficulties in differentiating between what is real and unreal due to inherited problems. Like with most things it becomes a matter of degree and circumstance whether this is truly a problem area or whether it is a natural defense. Excessive fantasizing and thinking of unreal things, having difficulty with separating reality from fantasy can be the product of certain drugs or medications which are prescribed, the use of street drugs and unprescribed medications as LSD, amphetamines (speed and other such agents) which may have been obtained by the child. Also exposure to certain toxic agents (accidentally ingested poisons as found in house cleaners, pesticides, solvents which may be inhaled or absorbed through the skin) can also be the cause of bizarre thinking. Rarely, they can also be due to some unusual allergic reaction to some food or even pollen exposure. We also know that a small percentage of the population have a family history of excessive paranoid thinking, problems in differentiating reality from fantasy and this is associated with a family history of schizophrenia. We may also see in some children where they seem to go from a period where they are very dramatic and have an active imagination and then continue not just to have the active imagination but will start wearing clothes that are inappropriate or bizarre or start doing other things which seem strange. The trick is to sort whether that child has an active imagination or is interested in dramatics and acting so it might be perfectly natural for them to engage in unusual speech, clothing and behavior for a period of time (a "phase"). However, if this becomes a total preoccupation, if it is associated with disorganized thinking, if they seem to have hallucinations visual or auditory or hallucinatory behavior (where they seem to be responding to voices or visions which are not evident to people around them), if they become unusually suspicious, if they start talking about weird things, have so-called "unusual thought content" and if you when talking with them feel that you are talking with them but are not really able to connect these are extremely significant clues. Another significant clue for somebody who may have a schizophrenic-type picture is that they seem to have no emotion at all. Like with many other situations it is not one particular symptom or sign that is significant but it is a cluster of the patterns that present and persist. When we refer to schizophrenia this has a wide number of possible disturbances expressed in thinking, feeling and behavior. As indicated **CLUES** include: the inappropriate mood, an inability to have some social awareness and relate to others in a meaningful way, extreme ambivalence (inability to make decisions), immature or regressed type of behavior and then sometimes hearing voices and feeling unusual powers within oneself or that some outside forces are directing one's behavior. All of these are sometimes seen in people who have schizophrenic-type process or schizophrenic reactions in relation to some drug or toxic agent as noted. Other problems might trigger this problem. This include such things as a physical disturbance of brain function that may have been associated with a birth injury or subsequent injury as in a bike accident or being hit by a car. The other thing to keep in mind is that some people who have so-called bi-polar or manic depressive illness as discussed in Question 18, if they get very manic may go into a period where they have paranoid and hallucinatory behavior as well as some of the other features mentioned. One other type of problem that is frequently not identified is if somebody has type of minimal seizure phenomena (so-called complex partial seizure) wherein there is a brief lapse of attention, awareness and mood and then this may be associated with some altered function like seeing things distorted, seeing them excessively small or large and then due to a series of events they proceed to have other problems including the schizophrenic or bizarre behavior described elsewhere. For more information about the types of things seen sometimes with complex partial seizures and associated behavioral and thought disturbances, you can find more information in Questions 2, 3, 7, 8, 10, 11, 12, 18 and 24.

There is a condition called schizo-effective disorder which is a combination of schizophrenic-like behavior and bi-polar illness and which also is frequently very confusing especially if it presents in a subtle form. The features are the thought disorders as described in schizophrenia as well as the mood swings associated with manic-depressive illness. One should be particularly alert to this possibility if somebody has some of the features noted and this is particularly evident in many people who have a lot "flair, creativeness, artistic tendencies" and have some significant deviation from the "average, normal" person. Now, this is not to be critical or say that these people cannot function and get along fine. The point is if these subtle clues are present, one should ask themselves "is part of this 'unusual' behavior in the child an expression of this problem?" One gets clues here sometimes by knowing if the family has similar problems or if there are problems in the family for example of excessive drug abuse, alcohol abuse, criminal behavior—one should make further inquiries. [Ideas on how to gather this additional information are in the Appendix in the history forms included.]

CASE HISTORY: NANCY

Nancy is a fifteen year old girl who at times was very dramatic and artistic and at other times very sullen. She also has been noted to be suddenly angry and when this happened she became paranoid. There was also an associated history that she had of problems with her attention and getting poor grades at school, though her parents and teachers both indicated she is very bright. She drove many of friends crazy because part of the time she was fun to be with and very imaginative, enjoyed play-acting, drama and painting. Then she would have periods of withdrawal and be undependable and difficult. She also was bi-lingual. Her parents had immigrated to this country from central Europe when she was eleven years old and she spoke Russian and English fluently.

When I first saw her she had had the "baggage" of multiple diagnoses and treatments. These included having been hospitalized, several months before I saw her, at a psychiatric hospital. This was for reports of suicide threats and because she could not be at school or at home without constant aggressive and violent behavior to other students, the teacher or her mother. In the course of her hospitalization she had had various psychiatric evaluations and some medication but never had a neurological consultation or an electroencephalogram. In exploring the history it evolved that she had had four of years of ballet training and was a promising young dancer. Then one year before coming to the U.S. an injury prevented her from continuing with her ballet. She refused to participate in any type of dancing after this. This seemed to be the beginning of a period of emotional turmoil for her. Also in the period after this injury rather than being sociable, friendly and out-going as well as interested in many activities and people she started having the fluctuating picture of sometimes being very at ease with friends and sometimes being unusually suspicious. She also part of the time would withdraw to her room and refuse to open the door when her mother would ask her to come to dinner or participate in some activity. It was also observed that she closed her shades at times during the day, started dressing in a bizarre fashion, including doing this bizarre dressing when she was going to school. At first this was regarded as just a dramatic flair and her parents did not wish to say much or do much about it because they thought this was just a phase she was going through. When she had more of this withdrawal behavior at times associated with the violent behavior described as well as the appearance of responding to hallucinations, visual and auditory, she was hospitalized. In the hospital, the history noted above was obtained with the exception that it was not identified that she had at times a bit of twitching of the right side of her mouth and eye and it was during such times that she became even more aggressive, violent and hallucinatory as well as unmanageable. The treatment in the hospital was Haldol (a psychotropic medication) which seemed to help her calm down, mellow her out, stop the hallucinations but she continued to have some of the twitching of her face at times and was continuing to be unhappy. She also reported frequent headaches which would be in the back of her neck and head, not respond to aspirin and come and go lasting up to several hours. The headaches were nonspecific except that they seemed to be more often associated with times when she seemed to be upset even while on the Haldol medication. She did return to school before I first saw her. She was doing even more poorly and the eccentric behavior and problems with attention continued. Also her schoolwork went from fair to failing. Only the violent behavior was rare—now—on Haldol.

To me she complained that (as she had to others) the medication was causing nausea and also that she felt slowed down by it. Additional history that evolved in talking with her and her parents was that her father had been a successful engineer in Russia and was beginning to do well in the computer industry here as a computer programmer. Her mother had been a doctor in Russia and was somewhat unhappy that she could not resume this work in the United States but was working as a nurse's aide part of the time. It turned out on further inquiries there was a paternal uncle who had a seizures after a head injury and that her maternal uncle had periods of depression in between which times he had been a successful member of a major ballet troupe in Moscow. (The clues that began to possibly be exposed here was a creative family who had also a history of depression and also a history on one side of the family of someone who had seizures which were attributed to a head injury—this sometimes can be true, that is seizures can follow a head injury, however, there are other times when

one will get seizures after a head injury because of a pre-existing vulnerability—familial vulnerability to seizures—and this should also alert one to
possible genetic problems. The element of the uncle in the family being a
ballet troupe member was also critical. This gives an indirect clue that one
has here somebody who is at the very least going to be extremely methodical, hardworking and compulsive in their training. This, of course, in
itself is of no concern. However, the indirect clue here is that there is a
high frequency of people who have obsessive-compulsive disorders among
those who are successful in ballet troupes as well as in certain artistic dis-
ciplines that require this extreme degree of discipline.

Examination of Nancy revealed nothing except a mildly abnormal
electroencephalogram and a history of mild asthma at times which
appeared to be increased with stress as well as seasonal allergies. We discussed the problem with her and her parents and came to the following
presumptive diagnosis:

1. Family history of pre-disposition to obsessive-compulsive traits.

2. Cultural stresses.

3. Depression history.

4. Schizophrenic features.

5. Convulsive disorder—mixed type—suspected as expressed by
    the periods of twitching face, rage and violent reactions and
    extremes of mood changes.

6. Allergic reactions perhaps compounding and aggravating all of
    these things—as reflected by asthma history.

It seemed probable that all of these diagnoses were "interacting" and
needed to be considered in a treatment plan. The best explanation of her
illness and its severity appears to be: a genetic (inherited) vulnerability
first triggered by stresses from having to give up ballet. This was then

compounded further by the move to the U.S. and further stresses associated with hormonal changes of puberty.

I discussed her problem with her and her parents and then suggested the following treatment plan:

A. Therapy sessions.

We arranged a weekly treatment session for Nancy with me for one month. At the same time arranged a phone conference with Nancy and parents once every two weeks. Also—arranged for the parents to see a therapist—counselor once every two weeks. After one month I saw Nancy once a month and kept in touch by phone in between. Also encouraged a conference with her school teacher, Nancy and parents. Assisted Nancy to get into some art/painting classes—an area she had interest in.

B. Adjusted her medication.

1. Initially she was started on Depakote (an anti-convulsant which can be helpful for both aggressive behavior as well as the abnormalities of the electrical activity of the brain which might contribute to her seizure disorder.

2. Navane, a tranquilizer-type medication which is helpful in containing the disturbed thinking.

3. Anti-histaminic—Benadryl on a maintenance basis. With this change-over in treatment as well as discussion and supportive care involving both her and her family over the next two years she made significant improvement. It should be noted that this was a very gradual process and involved both adjustments of therapy program and medications, and discussions with the parents and teachers. It also should be noted that after six months the medication protocol had to be complemented with Prozac which proved a helpful adjunct to deal with some of the obsessive-compulsive traits which she had exhibited and which history of was elicited as we went on in therapy. The

obsessive-compulsive traits were ones which she had not acknowledged and which her parents did not comment on until after a few months of therapy. Several of the obsessive-compulsive traits which gradually evolved in the course of discussing various of her activities related to her spending hours reorganizing her drawers as far as her clothing at home and the make-up on her dresser. Also she was spending hours with her make-up and this was just one of several ways in which the clear disturbing aspect of her obsessive-compulsive features came out. Initially the other aspects of the disturbed behavior were so profound that there was little mention made of this by her and her parents did not say much about it. Obviously many young women as well as other men and women might spend a great deal with personal care and so forth but if it reaches a point where it is disturbing one's regular life and interfering with doing many things and never done in a way that is satisfactory to the individual it certainly indicates a serious problem. Another reason why some of the excessive time spent with orderliness and make-up was not given due attention at first by her parents was twofold: first, they knew about her interest in the theater and accepted part of the obsessive traits as "just part of the interest in the theater", and secondly, her mother also had significant obsessive-compulsive traits and so was not inclined to even recognize let alone be commenting to Nancy's doctor that she was doing something which to a lesser extent the mother likewise was doing and these same traits to a lesser degree were disturbing her mother's life at times. The mother, however, had managed to compensate for these with these other activities. After three years she was getting along fairly well at school as well as beginning to participate more actively in a school theater group which gave her an outlet for some of her considerable talents. We expect that long-term supportive treatment will be needed at a less intense and less demanding frequency. Also as time goes on she will probably need less medication but continue to need medication as well as psycho-social support. She can be expected to live a reasonably normal life and is beginning to plan long-term even though she is still a teenager.

---

16.   Do you often feel depressed (sad, cry, no energy) or have you ever been told you look depressed by others?

Depression can present itself in many different ways. If someone is crying and tells you "life is worthless," and that they feel like killing themselves—most people would recognize this as being associated with depression. The problem arises (and this is even more difficult in children) when the first expressions of depression are vague and not well delineated.

Children with depression may have some of the classical "vegetative symptoms"—that is, they suffer from decreased appetite, decreased energy, constipation, and they sleep excessively. Or they may exhibit subtle changes in their behavior. For example, they might not wish to go to school or visit with friends or play games or converse as usual. They also **might**, for reasons that are unexplained, start paying little attention to their personal appearance, do poorly with their classwork, and **have trouble with their attention and learning, where before they had been good students.**

If you ask a child or young teenager something non specific, like "what's the matter?" they may give some irrelevant explanation, such as "I don't like my teacher" or "I'm having backaches" or "my girlfriend is getting too much attention from other guys." Also, sometimes the depression can present itself as a report of many unexplained physical aches and pains (viewed as somatizing by some and a way to avoid responsibility) and lead to an excessive number of physical and laboratory examinations and treatments.

Another even more confusing aspect of depression is when someone starts becoming excessively picky about their diet and says that various foods make them sick. The problem with these many manifestations of depression is that one should, **in a practical way—with the FEWEST number of laboratory tests and consultations—sort** out the **most likely cause** of the problem. This is where, once again, **appropriate follow up questions (to these 26 questions) can be very helpful and lead to an earlier correct diagnosis and treatment plan.**

If children have trouble with their attention, it is sometimes due to depression. If children have problems focusing on their schoolwork or remembering things, it is sometimes due to depression. This is an important point that is often overlooked. That is because if a child is depressed and is given Ritalin or some other stimulants, though this can frequently prove helpful in the short run, it is not the best or appropriate treatment. The best or most appropriate treatment is to try and find out if there is a psychological, social, or medical cause of this depression (or some combination of these factors) and treat more specifically.

CASE HISTORY: MITCH

Mitch is a fifteen year old boy who was referred to me by a psychologist for further evaluation of his diagnosed depression and possible ADD. In addition, he got upset and "allergic and nauseated" after eating certain foods. He was certain that milk caused him to have upset stomachs as well as getting unreasonably angry. Because of his food allergies, there had been an excessive focus upon and treatment of his problems with the idea that his allergies explained his depression, his behavior, and his ADD. Certainly, omitting conspicuously allergenic foods (for example, chocolate, dairy milk, shellfish and other foods) can be very helpful. However, this treatment is frequently over-emphasized and other treatments, which would be more beneficial, are neglected.

He was in the ninth grade, was able to do well on school tests (because he was bright), but was not doing well overall at school because he would consistently either forget his homework or refused to do it. Mitch was able to make friends with his schoolmates; socially, he got along well. He enjoyed playing high school sports and was on the school soccer team.

When I first saw him, he had been taking Prozac (40 milligrams a day) for more than a year, and was still taking it. This helped him deal with the depression that had been present before he started on Prozac—which was expressed primarily by his inability to socialize with others.

Depression, as we mentioned above, can be expressed in many ways. As we pointed out, it can show itself by an inability to socialize with others. In some cases, it shows up as feeling very inadequate and being unable to do school work, sports, or social activities in ways that were previously possible. In others it shows up as a disturbance in eating habits (either loss of appetite or compulsive eating in some), sleeping habits (insomnia or excessive sleep), chronic fatigue (feeling too tired to do any normal activities), or problems with bowel function (for example, constipation or pre-occupation with bowel movements). It manifests itself in many other ways as well.

While the Prozac helped him with his social life, and helped him with his moods, it did not change his ability to pay attention in school. The picture was additionally confusing to the referring psychologist because he knew that Mitch's mother also suffered from depression and was being helped at this time by Prozac.

When I examined him, he presented himself as a very strong, healthy and athletic boy. His examination was normal. Routine blood tests had been done by his family doctor and had been reported as normal. He was able to talk about his problems and indicated that he was upset about the fact that he would sometimes get angry or depressed, and then maybe be depressed for a few days. Mitch also casually mentioned that he's a perfectionist and gets very upset if things do not go as planned. In talking with him further, he said that "I'm doing poorly at school this year." This in contrast to the good work he had been doing at school before.

He said he couldn't concentrate and then was upset with himself and his teachers felt that he was not trying, because his previous record was so good. He said he was sleeping poorly and felt sad; he added, that his friends told him he had stopped smiling. The basketball coach had also threatened to throw Mitch off the team because his schoolwork had deteriorated so much. In response to this threat, Mitch stopped working out, started missing basketball practice, and let his grades get even worse.

Additional discussion with Mitch revealed that there had been increasing problems between his parents and his sisters. His **treatment had been focused on the use of Prozac** (an anti-depressant) and **avoiding foods to which he was allergic.** He needed to be involved in supportive family therapy. This was being entirely overlooked. As a result of this he had also started taking his medicine irregularly. A consultation at this time with Mitch and his parents made it acutely clear to everyone involved that the parents and Mitch needed some psychological counseling. Until this crisis—and his dropping off of the basketball team—the parents were trying to have all the treatment focused on Mitch. They wanted a simple, pill cure…and to blame me for Mitch's not being cured quickly. They would also phone in demands for treatment changes and then not be available or willing to call back to discuss his problems or make another appointment.

I indicated that the only condition under which I could only continue to treat Mitch was if he and his parents undertook some counseling to deal with family issues. His difficulties with his parents and sisters led Mitch to stop taking his medicines. This in turn caused a cascade of problems—getting depressed, dropping off of his basketball team, and starting to miss school. Over the next couple of years we gradually worked these problems out, with a collaborative treatment team. It is **often** the case that **until there is active collaboration between the** patient, physician, and counselor or therapist, and school, it is difficult if not impossible to make significant progress.

A suggestion to the reader: whenever you see a **change** in your child, a change from what is usual for them, this is significant. If the change shows up with regard to depression, trouble sleeping, change in schoolwork, change in dietary habits, personality change—any of these things should make you alert to an issue which may need treatment and which you should explore further. Just because someone is an adolescent and having changes does not mean that these are all "normal adolescent changes."

> **17.   Do you feel sick or allergic after breathing certain things, eating certain foods, or taking certain medicines?**

This is a very important matter. First, one has to try and decide, and be sure, that the sickness/allergy is from a medication and not something that is attributed to the medication. One must try and be clear that the child was not getting sick from some other unrelated cause.

Many times we have a situation where someone starts on a medication, reports a fever or nausea, and says it is from the medicine, "because I just took it." The next day, the child is taken to a pediatrician, who identifies a rash or says the child has tonsillitis, and it appears most likely that some infection has caused the symptoms—not the medicine.

This happens more often among people who prefer that their child's treatment be "natural;" to them this means getting medication from a non-traditional or non-western medical source. The importance of this phenomenon is that in the United States a large number of people are shifting to "alternative medicine," which includes Eastern medicine, natural medicine, herbal medicine, and other modalities of care. Because of this, when a child is given something by a "traditional" western medical doctor, there is great concern that the medication may be dangerous and cause dangerous side-effects. It is, of course, true that some medications cause side-effects—from western medical doctors as well as from "alternative" medical practitioners.

In any health care situation, the goal, of course, is to help—not hurt—the patient. If the problem is serious enough to justify any treatment, one must weight the possible benefits against the risks. There should be a discussion of this risk/benefit balance among the parents, child (to the extent this is possible), and the health practitioner. If the doctor doesn't initiate this, the parents should insist on such information.

Some children have times when they will report, or their parents observe, that certain foods cause them to become nauseated or upset. There are a small number of foods that frequently do generate allergic reactions in children. These are: orange juice, nuts, chocolate, and shellfish. Some children show up with unexplained learning disabilities and behavior disorders, including Attention Deficit Disorders, which are precipitated or aggravated by selected foods. At times, one is not even aware that the child has some sensitivity to one of these foods. Occasionally even the smell of certain foods—for example grapes or orange juice—will trigger headaches or confusion in some children. Depending upon the family situation and health professional that the child may be taken to for evaluation, this behavior can be regarded as eccentricity (psychological) or the evidence of a real physical problem.

At times, the report or observation is that the child gets sick just looking at a food. This, too, is frequently confusing. It may be due either to the smell of the food or to a "reflex" that has developed due to previous experiences. This is important to sort out because it can indicate either a true sensitivity or, perhaps, some learned behavior, which has little or nothing to do with the food or an allergic reaction to it. The critical feature here is that some people, including some health practitioners, get carried away with excessively restricted diets, without an appropriate type of evaluation procedure. (In other words, they may just do skin tests without doing any smell tests at all.)

Some children will report being unable to eat mushy foods or foods with a certain consistency, saying they get sick from them. This type of situation is more likely associated with some learned behavior. For example, a food that caused allergies may have been served in a "mushy" form. The child then will report "sickness" from a variety of mushy foods.

A simple diagnostic test, that you can do on your own, is to eliminate these most commonly problematic foods (listed above) and then try introducing them, one at a time, in a methodical manner.

CASE HISTORY: NORA

This sixteen year old young lady was referred to me for consultation and treatment of her multiple central nervous system symptoms and a variety of probably related other difficulties. The initial problems she reported were:

> times when the pupils of her eyes would become unequal
> for short periods of time

> headaches

> feeling sick or allergic to certain smells, including
> tobacco smoke, exhausts from cars, wet paint, and some
> perfumes.

The history of her evaluations and treatments—to just highlight the important areas—took six hours over three weeks of consultation. Over the next ten years I obtained much additional information which was very relevant, and in part, not revealed by her to me or her many other physicians due to associated emotional problems.

Nora's other medical problems included:

> mild learning disability

ADD Attention Deficit Disorder—diagnosed during elementary school

significant mood swings with irritability and depression at times and other times when she was extremely energetic

concentration problems at times

losing track of conversations

a sexually abusive stepfather

dropping things from her right hand unexplainably hyperactive thyroid (Hashimoto's disease)

gastrointestinal problems, with periods of extreme abdominal pain, sometimes associated with nausea and other times associated with diarrhea

multiple food allergies, particularly fermented foods

anemia

compulsive exercising, even though she reported poor energy at times

reported weight losses and gains of five to fifteen pounds within the previous two years. (For a five foot five, 115 pound girl, this was significant)
pelvic inflammatory disease

chronic fatigue syndrome

reactive hypoglycemia (over reaction to eating sugars characterized by weakness and other symptoms),

and assorted other problems. I should point out that her case is
somewhat unusual in terms of her large number of medical and psychological problems.

Her early growth and development was incorrectly reported as normal. Her schoolwork had been good in the years before I saw her, even
with her many problems. Nora's parents got divorced when she was two
and a half years of age and her mother had remarried twice. This led to
numerous household moves, school changes, and attendant problems of
making new friends. This contributed to some of Nora's conspicuous
emotional problems that were evident when I saw her at age sixteen.
Nora was living with her mother when I first saw her and her mother
was a practicing psychologist who was supportive of her daughter but at
the same time subtly demanding and controlling.

When I first saw her, Nora was pleasant, cooperative and said she was
having a good day and felt fine. Other than being a little bit under-
weight, she superficially had no abnormal findings in my general and
neurological examination. My examination of her thinking (psychological and cognitive abilities) revealed subtle difficulties with writing
words and spelling. She had a tendency to deny the existence of most of
her problems with relationships and her psychological problems. She
completed a medical history questionnaire which indicated many of her
physical problems but de-emphasized her psychological problems. She
also was working at a part time job after school and did indicate that her
social life was good. She was also sexually active which had led to her
having a pelvic inflammatory disease.

From the age of eight she had a series of evaluations and treatments
which included: allergy testing and desensitization, gastrointestinal
consultations (including gastroscopy), the use of antacids and bowel

sedatives (like Donnatal), sleep medications, anti-depressant medications, antibiotics for her pelvic inflammatory disease, intermittent psychological counseling, and consultation with a surgeon about the possible removal or her thyroid. Many of these treatments helped her for short periods of time and then lost effectiveness.

The question is—where do we start with a person who has all of these problems?

I had complete a very detailed medical history questionnaire. After this was completed I asked her additional questions and gave her, to take home, several additional questionnaires which focused on some of the medical, neurological, and psychological areas which seemed to have major problems. I also requested records from a number of her previous and current treating health practitioners. I phoned two of her more actively involved doctors and spoke with her mother, with her encouragement and consent. In addition, I ordered some additional blood tests, including one for Lymes disease and obtained an EEG.

The blood tests indicated anemia, a hyperactive thyroid, and low serum potassium (a blood salt that influences that transmissions of messages in the brain as well elsewhere in the body). Nora's weight fluctuations, and what subsequently was discovered to be a combination of bulimia (a condition where someone does binge eating and then to prevent gaining weight may do something so that they can throw it up or take laxatives so that they will not gain weight) and anorexia (a condition where one restricts the amount of food they eat excessively so that they can maintain an adequate body shape and weight), caused inadequate food, vitamin, electrolyte, and other deficiencies. Note that there is in our American society a considerable prevalence of adolescents and young adult women who participate in or have a problem with bulimia and anorexia. In young women and adolescents it may be as much as one to three percent of the population. In boys and men the occurrence of this problem is much less—it is estimated at one-tenth of what it is in girls and women.

These then manifested themselves as many unexplained symptoms, including mood changes, dropping things, weakness, diarrhea, and other things. The situation was then frequently compounded by her overeating and subsequently her using an excess of laxatives and enemas. She would then exercise excessively and report fatiguing easily. **She then came to her doctors (who rarely had any communication among themselves)** and complained about her various symptoms. **They were not aware of the fact that she had bulimia and then anorexia, because she was in a state of denial about these problems. She was able to divert the attention of her doctors by focusing on certain of her other problems.** For example, her weight gain was thought to be due to her thyroid condition and depression. Her excess weight loss was attributed to nausea, vomiting and diarrhea, which was thought to be connected with her allergies. The doctors would proceed to give her various tests and medications for her nervousness, insomnia, diarrhea—but never managed to address the total picture.

Nora's preoccupation with her **body image**—beautiful figure and appearance—led to her exercising to an **excessive degree** and the **unhealthy eating and purging habits** which were not revealed to her doctors.

Her EEG was very abnormal, indicating clear-cut seizure disorder. More of the seizure activity came from the right temporal region. This is known to be more often associated with periodic emotional problems.

I decided that I would try and prioritize my approach to further evaluating and treating Nora. Certainly it was critical to immediately relieve some of her symptoms. At the same time I knew, from experience, that it would be unrealistic and impossible to try and present her with an all inclusive diagnostic and treatment plan. This was because she had obviously shifted from one group of problems to another, over the years. She also gave some clear indications that her personality and problems were such that she was not going to be able to follow through with what I might offer her as a logical coordinated treatment plan.

I decided to focus on the following symptoms which were disturbing Nora. (It is important to provide some immediate treatment for most people with so many distressing difficulties, instead of just doing diagnostic studies and waiting until the results of this approach are seen.) I decided to treat her insomnia, sensitivity to smells, which contributed to many of her symptoms, as well as her headaches.

I prescribed Klonipin (clonazepam) to help decrease the frequency of her having attacks of unequal pupils. An unstable autonomic nervous system (involuntary nervous system) was a primary cause of Nora's episodes when she had pupils of unequal size. The instability of her autonomic nervous system also explained many of her headaches, diarrhea symptoms, sleeping problems and her sensitivity to smells. I also prescribed Donnatal as an additional aid to help her with her stomach aches and diarrhea. A week later, her immunologist prescribed Tagamet (cimetidine) to further decrease her allergic reactions as well as her stomach problems.

Her allergies—immunological problems—explained, in part, and contributed to many of her problems, including skin rashes, smell sensitivities, food allergies, and aggravated her emotional problems and her partial seizures. Her thyroid condition was another expression of her immunological problems. One month after I saw her, a decision was made by her immunologist and surgeon to remove her thyroid.

The reason was that it was contributing to and causing many of her other problems and could not be effectively treated with medications. This, of course, meant that there was going to be another few months needed to help her adjust to thyroid replacement medication, have associated changes in all of her other symptom complexes (for example, mood, diarrhea, energy, sleep), all of which had to be balanced in conjunction with any other treatments.

In the two year period before I saw her, as well as over the next ten years, she continued to see therapists intermittently. Depending upon the therapist she was seeing, the focus of her therapy was on anxiety attacks, problems attributed to childhood sexual abuse, her gastrointestinal problems (with questionable theoretical explanations), her rashes and skin problems (attributed by some to problems with closeness and relationships as a child), and her active sex live as a teenager.

She made a moderate amount of progress in the year following her thyroid operation. Her overall symptoms decreased in frequency and severity. She continued to have times when her hand would jerk and she would drop things from her right hand—a localized loss of motor control due to a seizure (called a Jacksonian seizure). Therefore we started her on an additional anti-convulsant Tegretol (carbamazepine). She was allergic to this and had to be switched to Dilantin (phenytoin).

She did better in school that year and graduated from high school at age eighteen, doing fairly well. At that point she began living full time with a boyfriend, had a job, and seemed to be doing better. Then there were more reports of vomiting, diarrhea, nervousness and weight fluctuations. At this point she was able to acknowledge that she had been shifting from anorexia to bulimia, without reporting this to any of her health care providers.

She got so sick that she agreed to voluntarily spend several months at a nearby sanitarium to try and develop some better behavior patterns as well as stabilize her medication program. She did better on discharge and did go into an outpatient program for bulimics. Nora also got a full time job, another boyfriend, and life was more stable for the next few years. At age twenty-four she decided to stop her Dilantin, and six months later started to have problems with her right hand once again as well as having more episodes of unexplained emotional swings (in part these had been controlled by the Dilantin). She had also discontinued her anti-depressant medication a few months before, as she was temporarily feeling better and also having problems paying for her medications.

With the resumption of Dilantin and a more active psychotherapy program, and continuation of her thyroid as well as other needed treatment, she is doing much better at this time. She now is working full-time, has another boyfriend and a more normal social life.

> ## 18.   Do you have, or have you been told that you have, rapid and unreasonable changes in your behavior?

Some children have what, at times, is referred to as a Jekyll-Hyde personality. (This comes from a famous story about a person whose personality changed from a scholarly gentleman to a mad scientist.) We see times when someone who is friendly, cheerful, relaxed and cooperative suddenly seems to have a switch go off and becomes mean, sad, angry, tense, unwilling and unable to cooperate with anyone.

This change may last for a few minutes or longer and occur at random times and without any apparent cause. It is frequently associated with a change in the appearance, facial features, posture, and muscle tone of the child experiencing this trauma. The point is, not only do we see a change in the personality of the child, but also see a change in the physical features and body language of the child affected.

A young girl may be playing dolls with a close friend—having done this many times before without any problem. And then suddenly, when the friend picks up the girl's doll, she starts screaming at her friend, grabs the doll, tells her friend she hates her, and tells her to go home. When the mother hears the screaming and the daughter's friend crying, she comes to the room and asks what happened. The friend is frightened, tearful and confused and says "I don't know what happened...I just picked up her doll to hug it and she suddenly started hating me."

In some young boys, this kind of behavior often takes the form of fighting and violent behavior, along with various kinds of anti-social behavior associated with this problem. A number of children exhibiting these rapid changes in behavior get involved with alcohol and other drug abuse at an early age. This, in part, is because they are so uncomfortable with their social behavior that they attempt to self-medicate, using alcohol and drugs.

CASE HISTORY: WALTER

Many children offer early indications that they have ADHD in the first two years of life. Without adequate treatment and support, a considerable number of these children end up in the juvenile justice system and then in prison. These children, shortly after birth, exhibit excessive irritability, crankiness, crying, and hyperactivity. They are sometimes described as "jumping out of their cribs almost before they can walk." This does not apply to those who are not hyperactive.

Walter's mother was worried about his hyperactivity and irritability when he was just a baby, ten months old. Her pediatrician recommended a diet with decreased sugars. This helped a little, but when he was in first grade, he was already fighting constantly on the playground and creating problems in his classrooms. His doctors tried several medications, including Cylert and Ritalin. These were not of any help.

His teachers and mother indicated that he appeared quite bright, grasped ideas quickly, and up until the fourth grade, got A's and B's in his class work, even though his studying and reading habits were poor and he had signs of a dyslexia with word and letter transpositions. At age nine his teachers discovered that Walter had been smoking and drinking alcohol occasionally as well as trying marijuana. Later information indicated that he had started using drugs at age seven. At age nine he was picked up for indecent exposure.

He started missing school and running away from home and by age ten had been sent to juvenile hall three times. As the last one was associated with not only petty thefts but assault on one of his "playmates" with a knife, he was placed in a residential treatment center. He quickly made a suicide attempt by slashing his wrists, which led to a psychiatric hospitalization.

At that time, the history of his being beaten by his father and having received head injuries from his father, was discovered. His father, it turns out, was a wounded Vietnam veteran who had problems with alcohol and violence. This included hitting Walter's mother with his fists and

attacking Walter's older brother with a knife. Walter's mother had con-
cealed this information from social workers and others until his suicide
attempt and hospitalization.

His psychological evaluation at this time indicated an IQ with scattered
scores in the 80 to 90 range, but good math skills. He was much lower in
verbal comprehension. As there was uneven performance in the testing,
the examiner thought that the tests were not completely reliable. Walter's
extreme moodiness, impulsivity and unpredictability as well as impover-
ishment in social and interpersonal relations (he didn't know how to get
along with people in a socially acceptable way) indicated a great risk of
continuing anti-social and future criminal behavior.

The psychiatrist who evaluated him at that time found him obviously
depressed and suicidal and diagnosed him as not having any organic problems but having the following psychological ones: conduct disorder,
aggressive, substance abuser (alcohol and psychoactive substances), and
borderline personality disorder. All of these diagnoses are frequently
applied to someone with this profile. These diagnoses have two major
problems. First, they do not consider the possibility of organic brain disease and second, they permit health professionals to delude themselves
into thinking they have an understanding of a problem by labeling it.

In Walter's case, there were many red flags (danger alerts) indicating
organic brain disease. These include: a father who is alcoholic and violent,
head injuries, a history of impulsive behavior, hyperactivity as a baby, irritability, rage reactions and assaultive behavior in fights without apparent
reason, learning disabilities, and head injuries—obvious evidence of
organic (physical) brain disease.

This, then, leads to the frequent—almost universal—tendency by
many health practitioners to focus their attention on psychological and
socio-economic issues and **not** think about and try and figure out what
else is causing the problem and what else might be done about it. If we are
mindful the physical causes of abnormal behavior—and evaluate and treat

these along with doing what we can with the psychological, social and economic issues, we can have a much higher success rate.

People like Walter, who are not treated correctly for their problems, create an enormous and disproportionate amount of trouble in their schools, their homes, and society at large—with thefts and violent behavior. Even when Walter was in a psychiatric hospital, his physical problems were not correctly evaluated and treated. The hospital discharged him with a diagnosis of conduct disorder, learning disability and other psychological problems, but neglected the need for medication to assist in controlling his impulsivity and violent behavior. Walter was sent to a residential treatment center, where he caused great havoc. The treatment there was behavioral training, group psychotherapy and the use of anti-depressant medications for his depression. He ran away from this center, got involved with more thefts, use of street drugs and fights, and ended up in juvenile hall again. This cycle was repeated seven times, with occasional periods when he was stable for a few days or so, before I saw him. He was, then, seventeen years old.

Because he had created so much trouble in the community and had been involved with numerous public agencies, a neurological consultation was requested and he was referred to me. In addition to evidence of a learning disability (though he could be described as "street smart"), he had neurological findings of mild organic brain disease. This was indicated by differences between his left and right arms when tested for reflexes and coordination. He also had, when I asked him to stand and place his arms out in front of him and close his eyes, a rotation of one palm externally. He also had a similar abnormality when I asked him to stand and hold his hands over his head with his eyes closed with an outward rotation of one hand. [Please see the Appendix for some additional ideas on simple portions of a neurological examination that you or your health professional could do with your child without even having special training.] These are simply practical ideas for screening but then can be interpreted with respect to whether they have any clinical significance or not—with your health professional.

He also had clear-cut seizure activity on his EEG. I also discovered that not only did he have periods of depression, but also he had periods when he was manic, as expressed by being very energetic for weeks at a time. During these periods, he would say he only needed three hours sleep a night (compared to his usual seven to eight), would eat less (in part because he was too busy to eat), and had grandiose ideas about developing a new kind of automobile engine—the world's greatest.

He did have some natural mechanical ability. However, when he would start telling examining psychologists about his ideas for creating a better engine than any in the world, they were prone to ignore it as a "crazy fantasy in a drug abuser" rather than realizing this was an expression of bi-polar illness (manic depressive.)

I participated in a team planning conference to try and work out a more effective treatment program for Walter. Through a private foundation we had funding available for a more intense program of rehabilitation and treatment than is usually available. Our team agreed on the following treatment.

First, he would be placed in a semi-controlled environment in a foster home which had experienced foster parents. This home used recovered young adults with similar behavioral and medical problems as Walter in a "buddy system."

Second, we instituted a new medication program. I prescribed Klonopin, which is useful for violent behavior, bi-polar illness, and seizure control. I also prescribed Tegretol, which also has the same over-lapping areas of effectiveness. (I used both of these drugs because in many case one or the other, by itself, is not effective.) He also was given iron tablets (Ferrous sulfate) for his mild anemia. At a previous hospitalization, he had received thorazine, a heavy tranquilizer, to control his violent behavior. Although this controlled his violent behavior, he felt uncomfortable from the thorazine (there were a number of unpleasant side effects) and he was less cooperative and less willing to try and work with the staff at this hospital.

Third, with his buddy we immediately had Walter start working repairing cars as well as doing some art work, which he enjoyed. After several weeks, he was able to start talking more with a supportive therapist and expressed interest in and started doing some high school work so he could get his high school equivalency.

There were several crises over the first month in this new program and then the situation stabilized. Over the next few months he began doing much better, but had several relapses from which he recovered. However, when he was permitted to live independently, at age eighteen, he returned to alcohol abuse, stopped taking his medications, got into a fight and ended up in jail.

Walter's situation was an extreme case, which was not identified as early as it should have been or treated as appropriately as it should have been. Many children exhibit rapid and unreasonable changes in behavior. When these co-exist with ADHD and learning disabilities, other important treatable problems, such as mood swings and neurological dysfunctions are often not recognized. **When these children have early identification and team treatment of their problems, they can frequently get along very well in life.**

Early identification is important because if neglected, it can lead to problem-filled lives (people who are unemployable, unstable and a burden on their family and society) and even criminal behavior.

19.	Do you have times when you have very high energy (compared to your usual energy level)? Or do you have times when you have very low energy compared to your usual energy level)?

There is a condition called bi-polar illness (formerly called manic-depressive illness) which affects approximately five percent of the population. It is harder to identify in children under the ages of 12 to 14. This illness first shows up in some children between the ages of five to ten, but most show symptoms during adolescence and during young adulthood. The problem, when seen initially, frequently is a very mild exaggeration of normal behavior.

For example, a child who normally sleeps nine to ten hours a night will cut down to eight or seven hours sleep per night. These children sometimes seem to be too busy to take time to eat the way they usually do. Their energy increases and they get involved in many more than usual activities. At first this may appear to be a wonderful improvement in their general health and behavior. If the children are able to manage these activities and maintain normal growth, there's no problem.

In some cases, however, a child will start losing rather than gaining weight, will seem to be unable to follow through with conversations or any work at school—even though the child was formerly a bright and good student. With adolescents, we find a very marked increase in drug abuse and sexual promiscuity as well as rebellion against authority—even more than is usual in their peer group. This change is also very much out of character for them. This change in behavior may continue for a few weeks to a month or two, and then the adolescent may return to a normal behavior or start going into a period of depression.

The depression is characterized by a marked increase in their sleeping, decreased energy, less interest in friends and a marked slowing down in their rate of speech as well as the appearance of looking depressed. They may have a significant decrease in self-confidence. Their drug abuse and sexual promiscuity may decrease; in some cases they will try and treat themselves with street drugs to control their feelings of discomfort associated with their depression. Normal adolescent behavior is frequently exaggerated in adolescents with bi-polar illness. We can differentiate between normal adolescent behavior and behavior complicated by bi-polar illness by asking two important questions:

1. *Is there a family history of bi-polar illness?* Psychological problems, drug abuse, multiple career changes or sexual partners are sometimes clues to undiagnosed bi-polar illness.

2. *Are there significant changes in sleep patterns, eating habits, rate of speech and scatteredness in conversations, and significant increases or decreases in energy?* In most people these changes take place in a period of a few weeks to a month. This period is followed by a period of normal behavior or a cycle of depressed behavior and energy.

CASE HISTORY: MAX

Max is a fourteen year old adopted child whose birth mother was seventeen years old at delivery and reportedly in good health. His birth father's history is totally unknown. Max was adopted when he was three days old. When he was referred to me, he had a series of reported problems and treatments over the past seven years. These treatments included consultations and brief treatments with two psychiatrists, two psychologists and a special-education teacher, helping him with his reading problems. Max's mother was uncertain about how effective these treatments had been.

The referring diagnoses by his doctors included learning disability, Attention Deficit Hyperactivity Disorder, allergies to certain vegetables and increased hyperactivity with eating sugar. He also experienced major sudden mood swings, and also had signs of an impulse control disorder. He had been treated with Ritalin and, before that, with Tofranil (imipramine) to treat his "Attention Deficit Hyperactivity Disorder" without any significant benefit. He was also using Tylenol for the treatment of his frequent headaches. The headaches frequently occurred before a period of major mood swings or explosive behavior—a clue to a medically treatable problem. These had both been discontinued, as they did not appear to help him—in fact, there was a question of whether he was having more problems at school and becoming more rebellious. Both of these medications, if used by someone who has an underlying bi-polar illness, my trigger manic behavior. This manic behavior is expressed by being more impulsive, having more problems with focusing, and inappropriate sexual and anti-social behaviors.

When I examined Max he was a pleasant, cooperative boy who was restless, continued to be talkative, seemed to have almost too many good ideas, and said that he could only spend ten minutes with me, as he had three appointments with friends that afternoon. When I asked him to hold his hands over his head, I noticed a slight outward rotation of the palm of his left hand and a separation of the fingers of this hand (technically eversion with fanning). This is an indication of a physical disturbance of the brain (extra-pyramidal system) in the portion of the brain that helps govern movement and posture.

His physical condition otherwise was normal. He did confirm and report the various symptoms noted above as well as indicating that he was experiencing some learning problems at school. He also was concerned about his mood swings and the fact that at times he was very sad and at other times happy, without reasons that were clear to him. When I saw him he was ebullient and said "I have no major problems at this time." Like many people with bi-polar illness, he said he was fine, and then, in the next breath, started describing various problems he had. And this is because, when someone is manic, they feel well and frequently cannot explain how they can feel so good and, at the same time, have problems.

He did indicate that he was having difficulties with his adopted mother and father because he wanted to stay out late with his friends and be more independent, but they would not permit this. For example, they would not let him go to a nearby Mall or do many of the things on his own that his peers were doing. He did admit to experimenting with alcohol and using some LSD and said that these experiences were followed by more problems at school.

Max was very adamant that the Ritalin was not having any effect on him at all. His mother thought that he might be correct about this. It turned out, as his mother and teacher informed me, that Max was not taking his Ritalin regularly.

My assessment of Max' condition was as follows. First, there was a power struggle between Max and his parents which showed up in different ways:

Max would say he took his medicines but he didn't; also, he would refuse to do some household chores and refuse to do some schoolwork in class. Second, he had mood swings, most likely an expression of a mild physical disturbance of his brain (organic brain disease) compounded by an inherited tendency to bipolar illness. Third, he had problems with various food allergies.

Although Max' history clearly indicated a combination of psychological, social, and physical problems interacting with one another, his **EEG did not indicate organic brain disease. (This isn't unusual.)** More sophisticated tests in someone with Max' problems usually do show abnormal findings. A test such as the PET Scan (Positron Emission Tomography) provides a visual picture of the utilization of certain nutrients (for example, glucose) by the brain and identifies discrete abnormalities in brain function that an EEG doesn't identify. Magnetic Resonance Imagining of his brain would probably be normal, however new research techniques in magnetic resonance imagining would probably indicate abnormalities.

Sophisticated neuropsychological testing (a series of very detailed standardized tests) would probably have identified subtle abnormalities in Max' brain function. Neuropsychological tests identify details as to problems with spatial orientation, timing, body image, fine motor coordination and other details.

I recommended a combination of the following. **One**, a very strong behavioral training program—to be conducted at school and with parental education about how to use this at home, also. **Two**, biofeedback training. **Three**, new medications—I stopped the Ritalin and started Depakote (a medication which is useful for both mood swings and increased cerebral irritability which contributed to his explosive behavior). The Ritalin may have helped a little with his attention but had a tendency apparently to precipitate more of his mood swings particularly his hyperactive and manic behavior, though this was not evident initially. Max improved somewhat with this program over three months time. As he was continuing to have bursts of anger and combativeness, I added Catapress (clonidine) to his medication. This is helpful for both aggressive behavior as well as mood swings.

One year later Max was showing continuing gradual improvement. It is important to note that his parents were more actively participating in his treatment, which was as critical as the school behavior program and the new medications.

20. Do you have frequent ear or throat infections?

Young children often have ear and throat infections during the first five or six years of life. Many of these children are given various kind of antibiotics at different times in their life (for example, tetracycline preparations, sulfa preparations, penicillin, Augmentin and so on). When these children *also* have difficult to evaluate and treat learning disabilities and behavior disorders, one must look further.

These children often have the following cluster of problems:

A. a higher frequency of poor nutrition,

B. an overgrowth of bacteria and fungi in their gastrointestinal system,

C. an increase of allergic and sensitivity problems with other medications; and

D. other immunological problems.

This group of children frequently need evaluation and treatment by a physician or a practitioner skilled in dealing with their immunological problems. Interestingly, there has been identified a group of children who have an obsessive-compulsive disorder syndrome developing months and sometimes years after recurrent infections, including streptococcus infections. As many as 25 percent of these children are reported to have significant improvement of their obsessive-compulsive disorder when treated with antibiotics and sometimes with associated special immunological treatments.

Therapy that only addresses psychological, educational, social, or even physical treatment measures like biofeedback—unless complemented with adequate treatment of the immunological problem, will frequently not be effective.

CASE HISTORY: GEORGE

George is an eight year old who was adopted at age one. He was brought in to see me by his adoptive mother because of he experienced episodes of dizziness for a few seconds once or twice a month. He described his dizziness as "suddenly feeling as if I'm spinning for a few seconds and then being okay." He was also reported to exhibit oppositional behavior at school and, in addition, he was diagnosed as having ADD. It turns out, as will be explained later, that his disruptive behavior (and poor academic performance) and restless leg movements in class which were taken as symptoms of ADD were not examples of ADD, but were caused by George's physical problems. Casually his mother mentioned a history of repeated treatment for "tonsillitis" and "ear infections."

It is important to get specific details when somebody says they've had dizzy spells—also to inquire about other questions—"cured problems"—like George's infections. For instance, we can ask the following questions:

1. Does the dizzy spell occur only with movement?

2. Has it just followed an ear infection?

3. Is it associated with double vision?

4. Is there some change in alertness or attention with or immediately after the dizzy spell?

5. Have other problems followed or been associated with dizzy spells or did the dizzy spells precede them?

6. Is there nausea before or after the dizzy spell?

Frequently this cluster of dizziness and nausea (and sometimes other physical symptoms) cause people to incorrectly assume that the person with these complaints has psychological problems causing everything.

This sorting out of the timing and associated symptoms is very helpful in identifying frequently overlooked problems reported by children who have attention deficits and learning disabilities. A detailed case history and examination of the causes of the dizziness can frequently help identify problems in the nervous system or vision which may have been incorrectly blamed on a "recurrent ear infection" or attributed to an emotional cause.

In George's case, he had recurrent ear infections, which had been treated unsuccessfully many times with antibiotics. Between three months and nine months of age, George had six serious ear infections. He also had some unexplained periods of four second spells of eye closing body shuddering, and unexplained five minute duration spells of crying during the night. The doctors suspected a type of seizure and did a sleep EEG when George was ten months old. The EEG was reported as normal. It is very difficult to be sure of small, subtle abnormalities in an infant, so George's EEG actually could have been interpreted as abnormal by a different neurologist.

When he was a year old, his ear, nose and throat (ENT) doctor placed and left drainage tubes in his ears to help clear George's ear infections. These tubes had been in place for a year and helped cure his ear infections. One of the problems of recurrent and severe ear infections is that they sometimes cause a small irritation of that portion of the brain (temporal lobe) which is adjacent to the ear infection. Ordinarily, ear infections do not lead to this problem.

When I saw him, George's adoptive mother and teachers reported that he was "oppositional" and non-compliant at times. That is, he appeared to be contrary and argumentative for no reason at all. In between, he was pleasant and a very good student. He also was reported at times to get upset—sometimes this was associated with his headaches—and then he appeared to get paranoid or "oppositional" after the headaches. Some people attributed his headaches to stressful situation.

His most recent examination, a year before I saw him, was reported as comprehensive and normal. The first time I saw him he was receiving Tylenol and Ibuprofen (Advil) for headaches. These were helping a little bit, but were not solving the problem.

His mother indicated that she was suffering from depression, which had shown up in part as headaches and irritability. These symptoms cleared after her doctor prescribed Paxil (an anti-depressant). Some of George's diagnostic evaluation and treatment over the previous two years had been directed to supportive psychotherapy for his mother and stress reduction efforts for him. This was with the diagnostic formulation that since his mother had depression and he seemed to get headaches and have behavior problems due to stress, that his problems were psychological and social.

My examination of George was interesting in that he was normal in appearance, and very pleasant and easy to deal with. He did acknowledge the symptoms noted above and with detailed questioning reported selected additional symptoms—but did not complain about everything like some "oppositional" children do. It is important to ask a large number of questions to get important information which would never be volunteered by parents, teachers, or the child—because they may not think of it or not think it is relevant. Sometimes what appears to be irrelevant areas of general history helps alert one to important areas of information.

I ordered some blood tests and did an EEG. The blood tests and the EEG were normal. In a second visit, as we did not have any adequate explanation for either his dizziness or so-called oppositional behavior, I got more details about George's problems. I had made the mistake of accepting the diagnosis of oppositional behavior as correct.

What had happened was that there were times, for example, when he was playing and would suddenly go off and seem to ignore everybody. He would go over to a place where people couldn't see him very well and spend time adjusting his pants. When a teacher finally came over one day in the playground and asked him what was going on, George said he was having trouble with his zipper. After the teacher saw that there was no problem and told George to get back to the classroom, George refused. This was one of many crises which were described as oppositional and defiant behavior. In another situation in the classroom, he kept crossing and uncrossing his legs. This disturbed the class and George refused to stop.

When I asked George for more details about these incidents as well as his being dizzy, he indicated that he was worried that his dizziness meant he was going crazy and that he could not control the movements in his legs and therefore was crossing and uncrossing them to "cover up" these involuntary movements. (It is not unusual for people to have an apparent obsessive compulsive behavior which is, at first sight, very bizarre.) It also developed that his dizziness only occurred with certain rapid head movements and was not spontaneous.

It turns out that George had developed a very subtle movement disorder as a result of the infections he had experienced long ago. The dizziness was due to a minimal disturbance in the integration of his eye movements in the base of the brain (brain stem). I was able to elicit a very subtle nystagmus (abnormal lateral movement of his eyes) with rapid head movement by having him bend over, touch the floor, and get up quickly. This is a simple clinical test to identify this problem. The picture was then aggravated by his having a mild predisposition to depression.

It's been known for a long time—even before the days of antibiotics—that many people who had strep throats developed one of two types of medical problems: either an endocarditis (an infection of the heart valve) or a chorea (a type of movement disorder involving the hands and sometimes the entire body).

George suffered from a mild form of chorea and an associated mild obsessive-compulsive disorder, which was aggravated by the fact that he was being criticized for being oppositional. He was not in control of his behavior. Also, it appears likely that his obsessive-compulsive behavior was triggered by a strep throat infection he experienced years before which disturbed certain portions of his brain. (It has also been discovered that obsessive-compulsive behavior does not respond to psychotherapy. This condition needs behavior therapy and frequently some medication supplement, until the behavior therapy has taken hold.)

I discussed my diagnosis with George and his mother, and later, with his teachers. We arranged for him to get started with a structured behavior program and also involved his mother and the school in that program. As he was doing fairly well with the behavior program—without medication—I decided to withhold any medication and he continued to do well over the next few years.

21.   Do you have frequent skin irritations or rashes?

A history of having frequent skin irritation and rashes is a good clue that should point you to several additional and related areas of inquiry and useful information. **First**, this of course is frequently associated with allergies. **Second**, it may reflect subtle infections. **Third**, it should encourage you to ask are these symptoms, the skin irritation, and these signs, the rashes, also present in other blood relatives of the child.

These phenomena should alert us to the need of getting more information about the above matters: the allergies, the subtle infections and the family history.

Findings of abnormal irritations or rashes on the skin—particularly if they come and go are clues to many different conditions. I will just mention a few of the **findings** that occur in children and adolescents, and if any of these are present, you should try and inquire further and contact your health professional about some further ideas.

1. Birthmarks—if they are changing, increasing or decreasing? These birthmarks are sometimes associated with abnormalities in the brain and blood forming systems. These are clues to types of treatment which can be helpful.

2. Rashes and itching may also be associated with some known or unknown drug use, unidentified mites (in bedding or dust), poison oak or contact dermatitis and exposures to toxic agents in the air or water or food.

3. Acne, which becomes a very big issue with adolescents and then sometimes leads to other psychological and learning problems due to concerns about it.

4. Agents in cosmetics, hair sprays.

5. Poor hygiene, fungal infections, lice, oral and vaginal infections.

6. Viral infections of the skin, which may show up also in the nervous system, AIDS (HIV infections), hives (urticaria) and eczema.

The point to remember with any and all of these is did these various skin manifestations occur before, during or after the onset of some problem with attention, behavior problem or learning disability? If they coincided with these in a manner that can be identified it gives you clues that you can pursue. Sometimes you can identify some very useful associated problems which may respond to simple treatment and in turn help solve the problem which may be of great concern to you (the parent) as far as your child's attention deficit or behavior problem is concerned. A child frequently will be much more concerned about the skin problem than about his or her behavioral or learning problem.

Evaluations that have been helpful or treatments that have caused problems in blood relatives **also** provide information that is useful. It may help you and your health professional be more direct in selecting diagnostic efforts as well as treatments that will work, or should be avoided. For example, it is useful to know that a parent or aunt or uncle was helped or made worse by a particular treatment or medicine. [Please see Question 20 for additional related issues.]

CASE HISTORY: PETER

Peter was eleven years old when I first saw him. He was referred to me by a psychologist and one of the teachers at his school. The reason for referral was that he had a diagnosis of attention deficit disorder, at times ADHD, minimal problems with coordination and significant problems at school with respect to having fights at school (occasionally striking other students) and doing poorly at school at times, even though he is very bright. The parents also, when they call for their first consultation, indicated that he had many allergy problems, which included food allergies, runny nose, itchiness, hives and rashes, at times.

Before I indicate what I found about Peter it is important to summarize some of the background history, which became available from the parents and subsequently by retrieving records from his previous treating pediatrician, allergist and psychologist. First, it became evident very quickly that his parents were very difficult to please. His parents came from a Middle Eastern country and both were professionals and both doing very well economically, with his father being in his own business. Peter was born in this country, but due to the parents' business and family, they had traveled back and forth to the Middle East three times in the previous few years. Interestingly, some of the rashes and symptoms that

Peter had, as far as allergies are concerned, seemed to be better when he was traveling in the Middle East. Then they got worse when he returned to the United States.

Information from his pediatric evaluations and treatment in his first few years of life indicated that he was hyperactive, fought with his doctors during the course of his examinations at ages 3, 4 and 5, had the appearance of being quite bright and was a management problem for his family at home as well as in a pre-kindergarten school. Before age 5, he was identified as having frequent runny noses, colds, several bouts of middle ear infection treated with penicillin-type preparations. I discovered that there was a family history of asthma, eczema and food allergies.

In the four years before I saw him he had had a number of tests to identify which foods or other agents might be causing problems (he had a couple of tests called the MAST test as well as the RAST test). These tests identified the presence of certain specific food allergies, which included allergies to peanuts, egg whites, oats, tuna fish, soy beans and some other positive reactions. With diet changes he had improvement of his eczema, of his runny nose and asthma and how he felt.

He also had received Benadryl, an antihistaminic which helped some for the runny nose. However, in the two years before I saw him, he was continuing to have some allergy symptoms, though they were less severe, as well as having continuing hyperactivity and behavior problems as noted. He was started on biofeedback training as well as a course of allergy desensitization—EPD (a relatively new type of desensitization treatment where certain injections are given at intervals of every few months over a number of years and this is helpful for some people in terms of desensitization). (It was too soon to know about the results of the EPD treatments, although it appeared they may be beginning to help. However, the biofeedback training was thought, after a few sessions, to have made him more hyperactive. With a change in the biofeedback programming, he was reported to have become a little better with regard to his hyperactivity, but he continued to have other school problems noted. It was at this point that the school was getting increasingly frustrated with him and his parents were feeling that he was not doing as well at school as he should be doing and he was brought in.

Examination revealed a good-looking boy of normal appearance and who was quite cooperative during the examination. However, he was quiet and at times did not want to respond much verbally. My neurological examination revealed a minimal amount of difficulty with fine motor movements of his fingers, but otherwise nothing unusual. After a while, he did start asking a few questions about various things around the office, but this seemed to be normal curiosity for someone his age. The EEG abnormalities were not diagnostic in any way.

Further discussion with his parents revealed that when Peter got interested in a project he would methodically pursue this project and have great concentration. It also became clear that he would be obsessed with certain activities and compulsive about following through on them. For example, counting things in his room as well as counting items in his rock collection was done in a way that was not reasonable. He became so obsessed with collecting rocks that his room almost looked like a part of a rock quarry. Another important point that came out of discussions with his parents was how good his memory was and that he enjoyed art. Some of the extreme disruptive and impulsive behavior outbursts and fights he was in—it turned out—were the by-product of Peter's not agreeing with/complying with his parents requests at times. Rebellious behavior followed at school.

My assessment was as follows:

1. He had a clear history of various allergy issues as noted, which, in part, certainly contributed to and aggravated his behavioral problems in terms of fights, impulsive behavior, as well as his variable attention.

2. Peter's history and findings suggesting that he was above average in intelligence and the variability in his attention as well as his hyperactivity was a function of his environment rather than a primary

problem with him, although that also of course was an issue as he would over-react at times to his parents as well as school.

3. He had excessively demanding parents and there was the evident power struggle taking place between him and his parents. An additional problem was that they had certain cultural expectations of him and although they were doing well economically in the US-California environment, they had not adapted to American culture. They expected him to follow cultural patterns and activities and rules that were Middle Eastern and in ways restrictive and inconsistent with his peers at school. This added to the problems.

4. Obsessive-compulsive disorder.

We had some discussions with his parents and with Peter over the next few months as well as a number of conferences with the school. He would do a little better for a while and then have another crisis, after which the mother, father or the teacher would be call me. One of the important issues that continued to be a problem over the next couple of years was their objection to and concern about his taking any medication. I recommended certain medications to help with his impulsive behavior and his being unreasonable at times.

The parents, for the first year, refused to have him take any medication other than the Benadryl, as they were concerned this would interfere with his learning and possibly with his creativity. Also, they would manipulate things with respect to appointments and with respect to the school by saying that certain insurance issues were not being dealt with properly. Specifically there was an additional payment due by them beyond what their insurance policy covered and which they had agreed to. It turned out that although they indicated that their financial condition was very good, that they wished to control the appointments by postponing or refusing to pay their bills, and using this as a way of making certain they would get appointments. This type of interaction took place over two years. Finally, by the third year, the parents were able to realize that they had contributed to the problem, i.e., the attention and behavior problem at school.

At this time they also began to accept the need for medication. They accepted both the need for medication (Prozac) as well as for more conferences with a counselor near the school. With the combination of an awareness by all of the parties concerned—the parents, Peter, the teacher and the immunologist/allergist (**about the way the parents were trying to manipulate various activities as part of their way of trying to adapt to this country**)—Peter made additional progress. Two months after he began seeing me for treatment the biofeedback treatment was discontinued. Other treatments were continued and then one year later he had another course of biofeedback treatment. At that time this was useful as a complementary treatment program.

Peter continues to make progress, but still has some problems with his parents, which are in part being dealt with by their loosening up a little bit on their restrictions of him and in part by his understanding what their needs are. Interestingly, when the pressures from parents and school are decreased, his skin symptoms, eczema as well as rashes, etc. decrease also. He has continued to need to be careful about his diet, which impacts both his skin condition as well as his behavior. His diet will continue to be an issue over the next few years and will have to continue to be re-evaluated periodically.

---

22.   Do you have difficulty with your sense of smell? Do you ever lose your sense of smell?

Children who have problems with their sense of smell frequently have had numerous infections of their ear, nose, and throat. Also, if children report losing their sense of smell on occasion, it is important to inquire whether they have had any temporary disturbances in their other senses, their thinking or their emotions.

Sometimes children will have a brief experience of smelling something strange—for example, something burning or smoke and with this, at times, will also have a peculiar taste in their mouth. This may be associated with other things such as feeling dizzy, weird, nauseated, having trouble thinking clearly, and occasionally being anxious or upset for no reason.

The idea to keep in mind here is that a disturbance in sense of smell or a report of some bizarre smell sensation may be associated with a number of other brief disturbances which sound weird. For example, somebody may say that they seem to remember some things but can't recall other things. At times they will seem dreamy or feel that they **have things reversed** for no apparent reason. At times their hearing may be affected in odd ways. They may say they can't hear something but actually what they hear is distorted or they hear things in a way that is different than what is expressed. Also, along with these symptoms they sometimes may act in a way that is unreasonably emotional or paranoid, or they may become excessively religious or preoccupied with trivia. What we are getting at here is that if somebody reports some difficulty with smell that comes and goes, and especially if it is associated with some of these other symptoms or bizarre behaviors noted above, they may have a subtle disturbance of a portion of their brain (the temporal lobe which) in addition to recording some of the sensations of smell, also has a number of other functions. The disturbance that is present in the temporal lobe may be one that is not only subtle but perhaps one that the person was born with and which, unless one explores with additional detailed questioning, will not be identified.

The nerves which pick up smells (the olfactory nerves) are the only ones in the body that are directly exposed to the outside world. Experiences associated with the sense of smell are among the most basic and primitive that we have and play an important role in our lives from our earliest years. Many of our emotions (pleasures, fears and ideas) are associated with smell sensations in ways that we do not remember.

Also, the stimulation of the olfactory nerves causes an activation of a primitive portion of the brain which then triggers not only some of our memories but also, in people who have had brain damage, but also various problems. Things that we smell, then, in certain circumstances, can trigger major mood changes, sudden changes in the taste of foods, anxiety, dizziness or even a type of partial seizure. Smells, in selected people, can also trigger obsessive-compulsive behavior.

CASE HISTORY: HOWARD

Howard was sixteen years old when I first saw him for consultation and treatment. He was brought in by his parents and was a bright boy who had done well in early elementary school with academic as well as athletic endeavors. When he was six, however, he was diagnosed as having ADHD. Between the ages of eight and thirteen, he was treated with Ritalin, with moderate success.

He complained to different examiners about smelling peculiar aromas, at times, which nobody else could smell. Also, he reported a number of symptoms of interest: peculiar tastes in his mouth which lasted for a minute or less, bizarre feelings of numbness over his body, feeling suspicious and paranoid (without reason), periods of anxiety and nausea, and other periods when he would feel dizzy and confused.

He was being teased by other students because he was so conspicuously fearful and anxious. Around this time Howard also became fanatically interested in religion, which contributed to his being teased even more. As a result, by the seventh and eighth grade his schoolwork began to deteriorate, even though his IQ and academic testing revealed him to be above normal.

When he was thirteen, Howard's symptoms began to escalate in intensity and he became anxiety ridden and depressed. He started banging his head on the wall at times to try and relieve his symptoms. Before this he had been on his school's swim team and played in his school's band. He gave up both of these activities as his illness progressed. (When somebody has a significant change in one's activities, it should be seen as a red flag to indicate that there is a high probability of some problem developing.)

This led to a psychiatric evaluation and, in turn, to an IEP (Independent Educational Program) evaluation to see if he was eligible for special educational services under the category of being Severely Emotionally Disturbed. The psychiatric evaluation also revealed that Howard's anxieties and fears were really an expression of his obsessive-compulsive disorder, with associated depression.

It was also noted that a lot of his symptoms, particularly his anxiety attacks at school, were triggered by and preceded by:

1. being touched

2. things related to sex

3. discussions of religion

4. hugging between other classmates

5. not being able to complete something.

All of these phenomena are very frequently seen in people who have subtle disturbance of the temporal lobe portion of the right side of the brain, a condition often connected with a distortion in the sense of smell.

He was made eligible for IEP and his school worked out a special program for him at home, while his psychiatrist treated him with medications including Haldol (a potent tranquilizer). This helped for a while but he became suicidal and Howard had a one week period of treatment in a psychiatric hospital.

We should note that until his hospitalization, most of his symptoms had been explained as being the result of Howard's ADHD problem. (In fact a psychologist had indicated that Howard would probably had scored much higher on his academic testing if he did not have ADHD.) As a result of the focus on the ADHD diagnosis, some very simple screening questions, which would identified other problems that needed treatment were overlooked.

After a few months of home schooling combined with psychiatric treatment and medication, he returned to public school. Even with a good deal of special efforts at school and multiple medication adjustments, he was doing poorly and his family requested his school do another IEP and have the school district pay for his going to a private school which had a special program for someone with his problems.

After many meetings and legal activities, the school authorized payment for one year of special private school placement. At that time, it should be noted, he was on a large number of potent medications, including Anafranil (used for depression and obsessive compulsive disorder), Lithium (used for bipolar illness and aggression), Haldol, Ativan (used for anxiety) and Cogentin (used to counter side-effects of Haldol).

It was at the time he was applying for the private school that I was asked to see him and determine what other treatment efforts might be helpful. His parents reported that he had been immature at birth and the product of a difficult pregnancy. He also had conspicuous allergies to many foods and the allergies increased with seasonal changes—pollens, etc.

Howard's many symptoms of trouble with smell, taste, and numbness mentioned above had been reported to his parents and to various health professionals. But, as mentioned above, the health professionals had focused on his ADHD problems and overlooked the significance of his other symptoms, which were also present as early as age five. These symptoms became more acute has Howard got older.

If my questionnaire had been given to Howard when he was a young child, many of the more serious problems that developed later could probably have been prevented, or at the very least, ameliorated. A good case history would have immediately revealed that when he was a young child his mother had been successfully treated for depression with psychotherapy and medications. Also, my questionnaire would have revealed other clues to the likelihood that there was a physical disturbance of his brain (organic brain disease) as reflected by the head banging, significant change in his personality and the features which triggered his anxiety attacks noted above. Also the questionnaire would have picked up the visual hallucinations history noted in the history which follows.

His physical and neurological examination showed a number of abnormal findings. **First**, he had a slight forward stoop to his head and neck while sitting or walking. This was probably a result of all the medications Howard was taking. **Second**, he had gained thirty pounds in the previous year and was at least twenty pounds overweight for his height and age. **Third**, his EEG showed a type of seizure abnormality (paroxysmal discharges from the right fronto-temporal region). This is of particular relevance since if there is a disturbance of a particular portion of the temporal lobe, this generates abnormal perceptions of smell as well as emotional disturbances and dizziness. It also increases vulnerability to being affected by smells.

During the examination, he manifested clear-cut disturbances in his thinking; at times he would look out the window of the examining room and become suddenly panicked or anxious. He said he saw a prehistoric animal crawling on the telephone wires, which scared him.

He also talked about some of the science fiction that he enjoyed reading. He mentioned that he had resumed his exercising and was happy about this achievement. There were other evidences of obsessive thinking and compulsive behavior as well as other problems with reality testing evident during the examination.

His major diagnostic problems were:

1. schizophrenic reaction with associated depression and—obsessive compulsive features;

2. physical problems expressed in part by periods of peculiar smells and tastes in his mouth, visual hallucinations and allergies. (Visual hallucinations are almost always an indication of some physical disturbance of the brain—not a purely psychological phenomenon; and

3. side-effects from medications—stooped posture and weight gain.

I had a conference with Howard's school teacher, psychiatrist, and parents. I recommended that they try to decrease the academic pressures on him, support his increasing physical activity (sports had been one of his great interests), encourage him to read in areas that he was obsessed with, including science fiction, and make two medication changes. I suggested adding a B complex vitamin with zinc as well as multi-vitamin with minerals. I also suggested giving Howard Ativan at least twice a day, regularly, to try and help him with his anxiety. He continued taking his other medications.

We had regular phone conferences every two weeks over the next three months and then once a month over the next year. There were some adjustments in his school schedule as well as his medications. There was a period of time, after six months of treatment, that I stopped the Ativan (used for both anxiety as well as seizures) and substituted Depakote, an anticonvulsant which has longer acting effects. After a year he returned to public school in a special program. He graduated from high school, although he had some crises from time to time. He then took a job as a grocery clerk and managed, over the next couple of years, to support himself and have very limited social activities. He did continue to need supportive psychotherapy and a lesser amount of medication and is making slow progress.

23.   Do you have problems with seeing or suffer from double vision?

It is important to correct problems with vision as early as possible. These may be a significant contributant to learning disabilities and behavior disorders.

Double vision is defined as seeing two objects when there is only one object in view. In other words, if a person puts a pencil in front of a child, and the child reports seeing two pencils, we have a case of double vision.

If the double vision comes and goes—for just a few minutes—it should particularly alert you to the need for asking additional questions to find out about some associated or other medical problem that may be causing the double vision. You should ask:

A. Do you feel dizzy with this condition?

B. Are you feeling spacy with this condition?

C. Do you feel sleepy or tired after the double vision clears?

D. Do you have any numbness associated with this condition?

E. Do you have clumsiness or difficulty with coordination?

Positive answers to any of these questions indicate that there is a high probability of some other medical or neurological problem.

Double vision, in come cases, may be due to strictly an eye problem. It can also, of course, be due to drug abuse. However, it is important to consider that it may reflect a disorder in the nervous system. Before your child gets involved in extensive prescriptions for glasses, an eye-muscle retraining program, or, possibly, eye-muscle surgery, it is a good idea to check with a neurologist.

CASE HISTORY: SAM

Sam was the child of a woman from the middle east and a father from Western Europe. When Sam was three, his parents moved to the United States with him and his brother, who was six years older. Both parents were well educated and quickly adapted to life in the United States. They both had satisfying and well paid jobs. They brought with them a culture that tended to hide many personal and medical problems. This made it very difficult with them to obtain information about their family's (grandparents, uncles, cousins) medical history.

They also were reluctant to share what they knew about their family's medical problems with their doctors. As a result of this, their doctors were not able to get pertinent medical information until they had established a personal and trusting relationship with them. And this was aggravated because they belonged to an HMO where the treating health professionals were rushed and were not able to establish a personal relationship with them.

When Sam was five, he told his mother that he was having blurred vision and trouble seeing at times. His mother reported that at times when he would have blurred vision and get anxious, the pupil of his right eye would get larger for twenty to thirty minutes. He then would say that his problems seeing toys or trying to read letters would just last for a short time and then go away. Sometimes he said it was like a blur or hazy. Then his mother noticed that at times he would have trouble walking. She took him to their pediatrician who checked him and referred him to an eye doctor. Both of the doctors said they could find nothing the matter with him.

Another time, Sam told him other that the right side of his face felt tight and that he was having trouble chewing. Once again she saw nothing the matter and her pediatrician could find no cause for this difficulty.

Sam went to public school, where he showed an aptitude for art work as well as classroom subjects. He also enjoyed sports, and made some friends. He also seemed to be unusually nervous with strangers. His mother commented that he would do very good homework or, at times, a beautiful drawing and then, suddenly scream and tear it up. He did this, he said, because it wasn't the way it should be. (He was a perfectionist.)

At times he had problems socializing with others and had periods when he would not want to go out or play sports. He also complained about unexplained aches in his neck, back and arms which would last a short time. He doctors found no explanation for these symptoms. Despite all of these problems, he managed fairly well in high school and did some part time work in which he used his artistic abilities.

After graduating high school, Sam moved to a nearby city and went to a community college, where he did well for the first year. In his second year of school he began having unexplained problems of anger and got into fights with friends, which was unusual for him. He also had trouble sleeping, was having spasms on one side of his jaw several times a day, had times when he would seem to fall or trip for no reason, became suspicious and distrustful, and unable to go into crowded places for more than a minute because he thought people there would attack him. He also had more times when he would seem to see things that were weird distortions out of one side of his eye.

He had so much trouble with his thinking and with his anger that he could not continue with school or his part-time job. He realized that he needed help of some kind. So he returned home and was taken to a medical clinic and then the psychiatric clinic at his HMO. After an interview with a psychiatrist, it was recommended that he be hospitalized and he agreed to do so voluntarily. Sam was admitted to the HMO's psychiatric unit with a diagnosis of psychosis of undetermined origin, possibly a schizophrenic reaction (a thinking disturbance with problems testing reality) or an organic brain dysfunction as a result of taking psychoactive drugs. He had a history of having used psychedelic drugs (mushrooms, LSD) in high school.

On admission to the psychiatric hospital, Sam was described as cooperative, oriented, neatly dressed, and smelling (from not having taken showers). He had trouble with giving a history and seemed both slow and confused. His interviewers noted that he denied having delusions and hallucinations but they felt he was threatening in his manner and was potentially assaultive. Also, Sam was very guarded in what he said. His parents, it was learned, had a history of depression treated with medication and an aunt who had some unknown type of psychiatric problem which was treated with electric shock therapy, which helped.

His physical examination and blood tests were normal on admission and he was given Stelazine, a potent medicine for treating psychotic problems with thinking, feeling and behavior. (Episodic incidents of problems with thinking, feeling, and behavior almost always have a physical basis expressed through bio-chemical/neuro-physiological mechanisms.) The Stelazine helped decrease his anger and his paranoid thinking.

However, he continued to report trouble with his vision, times when he had muscle cramps in his jaw, and occasionally difficulties with his balance when walking. This was interpreted (incorrectly) as a body delusion (a fantasy about his body) associated with "schizophrenic disorder." He was then given Valium (a medication useful for muscle relaxation and an anti-convulsant) which helped him with his muscle spasms and permitted him to feel sufficiently comfortable that they discharged him to outpatient care eight days after he'd been admitted.

Outpatient psychotherapy was started; when he became agitated after a few weeks, the doze of the Stelazine he was taking was increased. (He also was tried on a number of other medications over several weeks and as they made him feel worse, he refused to continue with the medicines.) The Stelazine caused him to feel more muscle cramps and body spasms and he got upset and threw his medicine away. He then, over one year's time, lost contact with his friends, stayed home, had trouble sleeping, stopped exercising, and gave up drawing. When he would talk with his mother or father, it was only to blame himself; he thought some terrible things he did as a child caused his sickness.

He didn't work, he didn't go to school, he spent all his time watching television, and continued to suffer from muscle cramps and neckaches. His father didn't understand what was going on, and urged him to go to work or do something, not just lay around. This just caused Sam to feel worse and get more agitated. A year later he was referred to me.

His medical examination was normal. His psychiatric examination revealed that he had problems in expressing himself, that he had angry and suspicious feelings, and that he blamed himself for his illness. His EEG showed clear-cut seizure activity. After obtaining baseline bloodwork, I immediately started treatment with Klonipin and Tegretol. My analysis of his problem was that he had a combination of schizophrenic reaction and convulsive disorder. **These were compounded by the cultural traits which made it harder to obtain some of his history.**

The **schizophrenic reaction** was **expressed in part by** his feeling **unreasonably suspicious**, blaming himself for all of his problems, and **feeling** that **his body was weird** and not working correctly. The **convulsive disorder—seizures—**were **expressed by periods of blurred vision**, **times** when his **pupils were of unequal size, periods of sudden confusion, periods when he felt a sudden tightening of his face muscles and when he had trouble walking.** This convulsive disorder problem is a mixture of what is called Jacksonian seizures (tightening of one side of his body, etc.), simple and complex partial seizures (times with blurred vision and altered mood swings and other times interference with consciousness).

The interaction between the schizophrenic type symptoms and the seizure symptoms created the bizarre behavior and symptoms seen in Sam. Clinically this can be labeled a schizo-affective disorder in someone with a convulsive disorder—both complex partial seizures and Jacksonian seizures. This being present in someone whose parents came from the middle east and Europe and who also had a history of depression made the diagnosis harder to identify. It is also important to note in his history that for a while the episodes of anxiety which were associated with a number of other symptoms—specifically that he was confused and unclear about what was happening, were not explored and people who spoke with him just took his word "anxiety" as meaningful and neglected to ask more detail about what the anxiety meant. If they had they would have gotten the additional history noted.

I also sent for records of his hospitalization and arranged another appointment by phone in two days and at the office in one week. Over the next month he had weekly visits and phone consultations between visits. During this time I adjusted his medications and also established a good relationship while obtaining a good deal of additional history of his and his family's medical problems.

Over the next couple of years he improved, went back to community college and part-time work. He had to continue with his medications and outpatient supportive psychotherapy at intervals of once a month.

24.   Do you have a hearing problem?

Early identification and treatment of hearing difficulties is very important. Where any question is present about a child's hearing, good evaluation should include both hearing tests by audiologists as well as good medical/ear-nose-and-throat evaluation. A problem that is present more frequently in children with learning disabilities and behavior disorders is that there is an incorrect assigning of cause of the hearing problem to either residual damage to the middle ear or damage to the nerve that conducts sound to the brain.

The problem, however, may be higher up in the nervous system. Specifically there may be a problem with the integration of the sound at the brain level—a child may hear some of the sounds/words but not be able to understand them due to neurological problems.

If children do not understand something, people around them may say something like "didn't you hear me?" The child frequently will respond "I didn't hear you" when they really mean "I didn't understand what you said." One of the reasons why a child can hear sounds and not make sense of them is that there is a physical abnormality of a portion of the brain that deals with integrating the sound with another portion of the brain that helps translate these sounds into meaningful words. This type of problem is one form of aphasia. As mentioned aphasia is a general term indicating problems with either expression of language or reception—understanding—of language. It has many different forms it takes, including not only a verbal spoken form but also a written form as well as non-verbal gestures and many other subtle expressions.

Aphasia is a term used to broadly encompass the entire area of language—reception and expression. The problem is that when there are small, subtle expressions of aphasia, they are frequently not identified and the correct treatment is not provided.

Another problem which is mistakenly thought to be a hearing problem can be due to a temporary switching off and on of the brain—a type of partial seizure which is associated with interference with attention, concentration, and comprehension. When what appears to be the hearing problem occurs for a very short period of time, or is associated with some report or appearance of either anxiety or obstinate behavior, we have reason to consider additional diagnoses. The problems discussed above are generally attributed to a hearing problem or psychological difficulties or lack of attention.

The point is that if a child does not exhibit unusual movements of his body, bite his tongue, or have other conspicuous expressions of neurological dysfunctioning, people do not consider the possibility of a partial seizure. The partial seizure in a number of cases is actually causing what is thought to be a "hearing problem."

In some children we see three problems at the same time: residual partial hearing loss caused by infections, a mild aphasia, and a partial seizure disorder. In these situations there is often a tendency to overlook one of the problems, which makes treatment less effective.

CASE HISTORY: GRANT

Children who have ADHD, conduct disorder, and oppositional behavior, are very frequently problems to themselves, their families, and the schools they attend, and are at great risk of ending up in juvenile halls and in state and federal prisons.

When I first saw Grant, at age fourteen, he had been a ward of the court for four years. He was from a mixed racial background and expressed resentment, without explaining why, about the ancestry of one of his parents. Grant was sent to see me by the staff of a residential center, where he had been living for two years.

His early growth and development had been reported as normal with the exception of allergies, frequent and severe ear infections, and numerous emotional and behavior problems. He had also reported hearing difficulties at times, periods when he was unexplainably nauseated, periods when he felt weak or sick for no reason, and difficulties with falling asleep. The staff at his residential center reported many problems with him, including frequent fights, poor attention, continuous hyperactivity, paranoid ideas, possible auditory hallucinations (hearing things), and learning disabilities.

The pre-residential treatment records included the following history: his mother is a severe alcoholic and lives on the streets; his step-father had been in and out of prison for six years for drug use, robbery, and violent behavior. His two brothers and a sister were in foster homes. Grant had been suspended from school a few times for aggressive and disruptive behavior as well as having a consistent history of being easily distracted, lying, stealing and shoplifting.

Due to his violence and rage reactions he had, on two occasions, been taken from his residential home, to juvenile hall—because he was not manageable. On one occasion he was then taken from the juvenile hall to a psychiatric hospital to try and help manage his violent and aggressive behavior, which was too threatening for both staff and other residents of his residential treatment center. It was at this point that I first saw him.

A psychological evaluation had been done several months before I saw him. In summary, the conclusions were that educationally, Grant had average intelligence but was testing below average. This was due to his poor social skills and inadequate planning skills as well as his poor organizational ability and social deprivation. He had little insight, poor impulse control, and a poor image of himself (which he compensated for with grandiose ideas). He had no confidence or trust in anyone and felt no concern about other people and had no sense or remorse. During the interview with the psychologist he switched from being depressed to becoming angry and oppositional.

A number of medications had been tried in the previous few years, including Vistaril (a type of anti-histamine and sedative) and Mellaril (a tranquilizer). He was taking Mellaril when I saw him.

My examination revealed that physically he was normal. He continuously fiddled with items in the exam room that he could turn, twist or screw. Part of the time he would respond and other times he acted as if he did not hear me or appeared like he might be intending to ignore me. Additional psychiatric interviewing confirmed findings noted previously by the psychologist. His EEG showed minimal borderline abnormalities—these could be within the range of normal for someone his age.

I discussed his case on several occasions with the staff of his residential home. Several things became acutely clear to me. The staff was interested in helping him but frightened by his behavior. In addition, he was able to manipulate the staff, which compounded everyone's problems. As he was a ward of the court, we had to go through considerable red tape to get authorization from the court for medication changes. While we waited for the court's authorizations, the staff became increasingly panicked.

The staff did what they could with behavior training programs, one-on-one attention and enhanced educational efforts. When we got authorization from the court, I added Sinequan (an anti-depressant medication, which also helps with sleep) and Depakote (a medication which is helpful in some people with aggressive behavior and mood swings). These medications were adjusted over several months, with a little benefit. There was also an ongoing effort to have him see a therapist twice a week at the residential treatment center.

Over the next couple of years he had transient periods of additional improvement followed by crises which led to his being placed in juvenile hall, back at a psychiatric hospital, and then with slight improvement, at another residential treatment, where he continues to be to this time. At this time it is still uncertain as to whether he will be able to function in society or wind up in state prison.

The entire subject of learning disabilities, behavior problems, and ADD and ADHD is extremely important in our society. As we have mentioned there are a very significant group of children and adolescents who have learning disabilities and emotional problems. Some conservative estimates indicate that at least twenty percent of the school population kindergarten through twelfth grade have a significant emotional problem which has a quite important associated learning disability. It is also well-recognized that a large percentage of those people who wind up in juvenile halls, state prisons or at the very least are a burden and problem to themselves and society have learning disabilities and emotional problems. It is also agreed that the earlier we can help more of this group the better it will be for all concerned. **It may sound a little simplistic but there is wide agreement that a variety of individualized programs which are in place around the United States can be helpful and these can be tailored to the local needs.** It is also agreed that **many of these programs can be successfully expanded without a great increase expenditures.**

Let me repeat that it is this group of children with the learning disabilities and emotional problems who are the source of the largest grief and problem to our society and this is the group who in the early school years have a better chance of being helped effectively.

One of Grant's problems over many years was that he would not listen to his teachers, counselors or other children at foster homes where he had been. He had been abused and beaten by both his mother and her boyfriends in the years before he became a ward of the court. It became a very difficult task for interested counselors and teachers at the residential treatment center to decide, in their own minds, whether Grant was having a problem hearing or was just ignoring them and being what they viewed as oppositional.

The same mechanisms that were discussed in the discussion of smells (Question 22) are at work in the matter of hearing. In Grant's situation, we had this very extensive history of both physical as well as psychological abuse over many years. This led to his developing the behavior patterns—including hearing and seeing messages from others in a distorted way and reacting in an anti-social manner.

---

25.   Do you have any problems with your sense of TASTE?

Sometimes children report that things taste weird or strange. Occasionally they will say that they cannot taste something or that too many things taste "terrible." The significance of this is that it is an indication that the child's perception or awareness is, at times, either altered or exaggerated. [Please see Question 22 for ideas associated with problems of smell and taste.]

This should alert one to ask additional questions about the child's other senses. **A report of a problem with one sense, especially taste and smell, is frequently associated with other problems, such as an emotional difficulty or a feeling of being out of contact with their friends and family.** (The senses include: smell, sight, hearing, taste, and feeling/touch.) **Occasionally a child will report a metallic taste...for example, like a penny—which may last for a few seconds to a minute and then gradually clear up.**

Children frequently have difficulty in describing and expressing what their sensations are. A child's problem with taste is frequently associated with reported problems in the sense of smell (discussed in question 22) and altered touch sensation. (If a child is touched, he says either he doesn't feel anything or reports a minimal response to painful stimuli.)

The sense of taste is frequently temporarily altered by infections; also, it may be altered by rare tumors of the brain or diseases of the blood. Reports of an altered sense of taste can occur with depression, gastrointestinal absorption problems, and dietary deficiencies. [If your child has any of these symptoms, please refer to Questions 2, 3, 7, 8, 10, 11, 12, 18, and 22 for additional information.]

CASE HISTORY: ANNIE

Annie was fourteen when she was first referred to me for a neurological consultation. Her history was a complicated one. She had reported many food sensitivities; sometimes these sensitivities were associated with an upset stomach and a hysterical reaction. She also said there were times when it felt like she had the taste of a penny in her mouth...and then would feel weird. The precipitating factor for her being referred to me was that she had fainted on two different occasions in the previous month, without any known reason.

A quick review of her history by her parents revealed that **she had been** perfectly **fine until age seven**, when **she started to become a disciplinary problem in school and at home**. Also, even though she had been enjoying and doing well at school, after she turned seven her work there gradually began to slip. Educational testing proved normal; she didn't have a learning disability. It was therefore thought her problems were emotional and this led to efforts at counseling with her and her parents, which was not effective.

She continued to have problems, which showed up as marijuana abuse, followed by alcoholism (by age eleven) and a pregnancy at age thirteen, which was terminated by a therapeutic abortion. Through all of this her parents tried to follow recommendations by a variety of professionals, but nothing helped. Annie's general examination, by her pediatrician, continued to be normal. **The bizarre report of tasting a penny in her mouth and being hysterical at times, being obstinate, unreasonable and confused, were all attributed to behavior problems and then substance abuse.** She had had a two week period of treatment in a psychiatric hospital, in an effort to help her with her behavioral and drug abuse problems. This was followed by occasional visits to Alcoholics Anonymous.

When I saw her she was a little guarded but tried to be cooperative. Detailed questioning revealed that her feelings of being "weird," confused, or angry, sometimes associated with a sensation of metallic taste—came briefly and on a number of occasions, without her having used any drugs. Of course with her history of drug abuse, nobody believed her. There was a tendency to not pay much attention to what she said as far as her symptoms were concerned.

Her physical and neurological examination were normal, except for her EEG. Annie's EEG had evidence of definite seizure activity coming from her right temporal region (a portion of the brain which has to do with emotions, spatial awareness, and perceptions of taste and smell). Because of her history and the localized EEG abnormalities, we obtained a magnetic resonance imaging of her head—a test to visualize the brain structure. This showed a small deep-seated probably non-malignant tumor of her brain, at the uncus (tip of the temporal lobe of the brain). We know that tumors in this area can and usually do cause attacks of peculiar tastes, smells, and associated bizarre behavior.

I discussed the findings with Annie and her parents and recommended surgery. She had a successful removal of a meningioma, a non-malignant tumor of the brain. She did need medications to control seizures as well as some psychotherapy, but within six months returned to close to normal behavior. Over the next eight years, she has continued to do well at school, socially, and no longer has a problem with alcohol or drug abuse. We can expect that she will continue to do well throughout her life.

The lessons to be learned here are that: one, children's **personalities do not suddenly change without a clear-cut reason; and two, one should try and listen, and go into as much detail as possible, about the history of a child's symptoms, no matter how bizarre they may seem.**

> **26.   Are you very sensitive to pain or touch? Do you have any other unusual responses to pain or touch?**

Usually a child who over-reacts—that is, reports great pain or distress with small injuries or illnesses that appear "minor"—is more that just complaining. The child frequently has a hyper-sensitive nervous system. The child's perceptions of these stimulations is more acute than the average child's. Then, depending upon the way they were brought up, this behavior may be slightly subdued or lead to a number of secondary problems.

For example, a child who is brought up in a family that will not acknowledge that he or she may be feeling things or suffering distress more intensely that the average child, may have difficulties. The child may withdraw into paranoid behavior or have difficulties in playing with other children and interacting with adults. The child will think to himself "I'm having difficulties and my parents and teachers don't believe me and don't understand me."

This concept—that a person has an unusual reaction to pain that has a physical basis—is frequently not recognized by parents, teachers and health professionals and must be kept in mind at all times. Hypersensitivity to pain is sometimes an inherited (genetic)—not a "learned"—response. Too often, people assume that these reactions are due to some purely psychological source—for example, wanting more attention. This often leads to the child with the affliction being criticized or punished.

If a child reports little or no pain in situations where most people do experience pain, this is also a very important clue of an inherited nervous system with other possible problems. This is true unless the culture of the child is one—training and requiring—avoiding expression of "painful emotions."

What we are dealing with here is an incorrect interpretation or lack of understanding of underlying mechanisms by most health professionals and educators. There is a great deal of misinformation which has been presented to the public by health professionals (including psychologists, psychiatrists, and neurologists). They have popularized certain simplistic notions—analogous to arguing that the earth is flat—which we now know are not correct. In essence, these notions lead them away from considering the physical components of many symptoms.

CASE HISTORY: MICKEY

This seven year old boy was referred to me by a group of people, which included his pediatrician, psychologist, and immunologist. He had many problems: sensitivity to pain and touch, learning disabilities, food allergies, ADD, obsessive compulsive behavior and occasionally would masturbate in classroom or public situations, which was distressing to him and all involved. (It is most unusual for a child this age to masturbate.)

When I saw him he was taking Ritalin, which helped a little with his ADD problem. He also had been on a special diet, which eliminated artificial colorings, fast acting sugars, and milk and cheese. In addition, he was having desensitization treatments by his allergist and immunologist.

Mickey's mother had a long labor and at birth he had a little trouble breathing and was not as active as normal. He had an APGAR score of seven out of a possible ten. (An APGAR score is a standardized measurement of certain normal functions at birth, including breathing, movement and so on.) In his first few years of development, he had surgical treatment of an eye muscle imbalance, as well as tubes in his ears for six months for treatment of recurrent ear infections.

Then, at age three and a half, his growth and development became closer to normal and he started showing signs of being very bright. However, he had a variable and disturbing sensitivity to touch and also sensitivity to loud noises. His bowel and bladder training seemed to go well, except there was a persistence of some nocturnal bed wetting. For about six months, when he was four years of age, he was given Tofranil (Imipramine), to help control his nocturnal bed wetting.

When I saw him, at age seven, Mickey's immunologist was convinced that the most important treatment was to help alleviate his allergies (using diet and desensitization methods). Mickey's psychologist believed in the centrality of the role of biofeedback and behavior training. Mickey's pediatrician was very interested in cooperating, but felt she had nothing more to offer than general medical care. His teachers wanted him to increase his Ritalin, to deal with his ADD and help him with other learning problems. They also wanted him to have speech therapy because he had some problems with articulation and identifying simple words.

His school's special education coordinator was the only one aware of the multiple and somewhat conflicting treatment efforts Mickey was undergoing. She consulted with me at the time of the referral and indicated the need to coordinate the treatment efforts and find more effective ones. His dedicated parents had been pushed in so many different directions by various consulting experts that they were frantic and frustrated by their inability to get any results.

When I examined Mickey, with both of his parents present, he was a pleasant boy who was somewhat small for his age. He was wearing glasses which corrected his vision satisfactorily. Although cooperative, he talked a lot and was quite anxious during the examination. His fantasies, as expressed during the examination, were very unusual and perhaps a little bizarre.

He had a little clumsiness with fine movements of his fingers and a slight lisp and stutter when talking. When checking his muscles and skin in his arms and legs, he withdrew as if pained or afraid. This reaction cleared promptly when I took my hands away. His EEG had some borderline abnormalities.

At this point, I sent for records from other examining and treating physicians, from psychologists, and from the school where he had been for the last few years. His parents also provided me with some records of previous evaluations. To find out what was going on in this complicated case, I also obtained authorizations to speak with the others involved in his treatment. His mother had indicated that the special education coordinator at his school had the best overview of what was taking place, so I phoned the coordinator.

Unusual sensitivity to touch—especially when it is associated with multiple allergies and obsessive compulsive behavior—is often an indicator that a problem with the autonomic nervous system may exist, and in some cases is connected with brain damage. (There are very well known experiments with animals that indicate an imbalance between the chemicals that control the autonomic nervous system cause a marked increase in touch sensitivity.)

There is a well demonstrated association between obsessive compulsive behavior and anatomical/neurophysiological disturbances in the brain. These same disturbances are also frequently associated with sensitivity to touch.

After I had reviewed some 200 pages of Mickey's records, which arrived over the next month, and discussed his problems further with the referring professionals and the school coordinator, we formed a small team of involved people to work with him. We decided on a coordinated approach. This involved several face-to-face conferences between parents, Mickey's teachers, and the others involved in his treatment. This was supplemented by regular phone conferences and the exchange of summary reports on what we were doing.

This approach enabled us to select Mickey's target symptoms (primary problems) and major strengths to work on together. Our treatment involved the following areas:

Biological

allergy treatments

medications to help with his sensitivity and obsessive compulsive behavior and masturbation in public

Psychological
behavior and reward training at school and home counseling for his parents—including assistance in decreasing the number of multiple professionals used in treatment

Social
assistance with real life appropriate behavior at school and at home

Academic
speech therapy

special reading and math assistance

computer skills

Administrative
one of his teachers agreed to be the primary coordinator of his total program

the treatment team agreed together to try and greatly limit the number of special appointments and after school activities involved with medical and rehabilitative-type treatments.

These efforts were focused on supporting Mickey's strengths, his interests, his hobbies and to assist his parents with home behavior training techniques to deal with this obsessive-compulsive behavior. The point was that it was and is very important not to overwhelm the child and parents with an excess number of "therapeutic interventions" even though they might seem appropriate and the family and others involved might be willing and able to try and pursue these.

Again, let me emphasize that **too much "intervention and treatment," especially if the dosage and timing are not carefully managed, can backfire.**

Three years later Mickey was getting along much better at school, doing grade level work in all but mathematics, and socializing in a more satisfactory manner. There were, of course, a number of ups and downs as we proceeded. His allergies were controlled as were most of his obsessive compulsive symptoms—as long he continued with his medications and the rest of the program.

Appendix A

The 26-Question Questionnaire

PARENTS: THIS FORM TO BE COMPLETED **FIRST** WITH CHILD
NAME:_____
DATE:_____

EVALUATING YOUR CHILD: 26 KEY QUESTIONS

1. At times are you unable to pay attention for more than 3 to 5 minutes?   !Yes   !No

2. Do you space out? Do people tell you that sometimes you have a blank look or pale look on your face?   !Yes   !No

3. Do you daydream? Do people tell you that you have a staring expression on your face?   !Yes   !No

4.   Do you get upset when things you have   !Yes   !No
      organized get messed up?

5.   Do you ever feel suspicious of others (paranoid)   !Yes   !No
      for no reason?

6.   Do you ever do the same things over and over,   !Yes   !No
      with or without being aware of
      what you are doing?

7.   Do you become suddenly angry for no reason?   !Yes   !No

8.   Have you been getting into   !Yes   !No
      physical fights or yelling fights?

9.   Do you have problems in any of these: !Yes   !No
      reading, writing, math (arithmetic),
      reversing numbers or letters or
      lining numbers up in lines for addition?

10.   Do you ever become confused when   !Yes   !No
      you are trying to think?

11.   Even when you are paying attention,   !Yes   !No
      do you ever have trouble understanding
      what is going on?

12.   Do you have a hard time remembering things   !Yes   !No
      that have happened to you or things
      people have said to you?

13. Do you have poor ability to make friends or   !Yes   !No
     are you fearful of making friends?

14. Do you ever have ideas that keep   !Yes   !No
     going through your head?

15. Do you fantasize or think about unreal things   !Yes   !No
     a lot of the time? Can you tell the difference
     between what is real and what is unreal?

16. Do you often feel very   !Yes   !No
     depressed (sad, cry, no energy) or have you
     ever been told you look depressed by others?

17. Do you feel sick or allergic after   !Yes   !No
     breathing certain things, eating certain foods,
     or taking certain medicines?

18. Do you have, or have you been told that   !Yes   !No
     you have, rapid and unreasonable changes
     in your behavior?

19. Do you have times when you have **very** high   !Yes   !No
     energy (compared to your usual energy level)?
     Or do you have times when you have **very**
     low energy (compared to your usual energy level)?

20. Do you have frequent ear or throat infections?   !Yes   No

21. Do you have frequent skin irritations or rashes? !Yes   !No

22.   Do you have difficulty with your sense of smell?   !Yes   !No
      Do you ever lose your sense of smell?

23.   Do you have problems with seeing or   !Yes   !No
      suffer from double vision?

24.   Do you have a hearing problem?   !Yes   !No

25.   Do you have any problems with   !Yes   !No
      your sense of taste?

26.   Are you very sensitive to pain or touch?   !Yes   !No
      Do you have any other unusual responses to
      pain or touch?

Ask your child to answer these 26 questions. "YES" answers very often indicate
an <u>OVERLOOKED MEDICAL PROBLEM</u>, which can be helped. The medical
problem (or problems) frequently require a <u>COMBINATION</u> of treatments.
These are education, diet, medication and other treatments.

Appendix B

Central Nervous System Symptoms Questionnaire

NAME: _____ DATE: _____

CENTRAL NERVOUS SYSTEM SYMPTOMS

> If you **answer yes** to a question please **add additional information**. Do so on a separate piece of paper and identify it by the question number. [*ex. #1—yes I get peculiar tastes that last about 10 seconds—they only occur when I am ready to fall asleep.*]

A.   Have you ever experienced any of the following?

1.   A peculiar taste lasting 1 minute or less?   / YES / NO
      (Is the taste: *circle which ones*—bitter,
      sour burning, metallic or other)

2.   Sudden peculiar aromas (smells or odors) lasting   / YES / NO
      1–2 minutes or less? (Is it burning or other?)

3.   Suddenly see lights in   / YES / NO
      one part of your field of vision?

4.   Do things seem to be unusually small for   / YES / NO
      a few seconds to a few minutes?

5.   Do things seem to be unusually large   / YES / NO
      for a few seconds to a few minutes?

6.   Get an unusual sudden tightness of   / YES / NO
      one side of your mouth or jaw?

7.   Your head and neck seem to turn to   / YES / NO
      one side without reason?

8.   You get a *sudden* numbness of   / YES / NO
      one part of your face or body?

9.   Get *unexplained* chest pains?   / YES / NO

10.   You get *sudden* nausea for   / YES / NO

11.   You get *unexplained* stomach pains?   / YES / NO

12.   Episodes of sudden pain in your   / YES / NO
      abdomen, head, heart or other places
      which clears within a few minutes?

13. Get *unexplained* sensations in
    sensations that don't make sense,
    but clear after a short period of time?   / YES / NO

14. Have other bizarre sensations of
    tingling or feeling strange in some
    other parts of your body which
    clears fairly quickly?   / YES / NO

15. You get *suddenly* angry for no apparent reason?   / YES / NO

16. You feel suspicious or paranoid *without* a reason?   / YES / NO

17. You have *unexplained* period of happiness?   / YES / NO

18. You have *unexplained* periods of sadness?   / YES / NO

19. Do you have times when you are
    suddenly anxious or fearful and
    you don'tknow why?   / YES / NO

20. Are there times when you feel dizzy or
    you feel as if things around you are
    spinning for a few seconds?   / YES / NO

21. Do you get a *sudden* flushing or
    paleness of your face?   / YES / NO

22. Do you get a *sudden* rubbing or
    fumbling movements of your hands?   / YES / NO

23.   Do you fall for *no* reason?   / YES / NO

24.   Do you have blackouts?   / YES / NO
      (*if yes, how long do they last?*)

25.   Do you act *(or have been told that you act)* as if   / YES / NO
      you were searching for something or
      trying to locate yourself in space?

26.   Are there times when you are unaware of   / YES / NO
      who you are or are unaware of your surroundings?

27.   Do you have times when you seem to be in   / YES / NO
      a dreamy state when you will have
      a far away feeling and then it clears within
      a few minutes or less?

28.   Do you have periods of decreased or   / YES / NO
      altered consciousness?
      (*ex. a feeling of being detached from
      where you are or what's happening*)

29.   Do you have episodes of *involuntary* urination?   / YES / NO

30.   Do you loose control of your bowels?   / YES / NO
      (*daytime or nighttime*)

31.   Sudden aggressive activity?   / YES / NO
      (*unprovoked fighting and/or
      attacking—physical and/or verbal*)

32. Walking, wandering or   / YES / NO
     driving around for *no* reason?

33. Have *sudden* muscle spasms or jerking?   / YES / NO

34. Talk at length or get into   / YES / NO
     verbal arguments for *no* clear reason?

35. Do you have a history of head injuries?   / YES / NO
     (if yes, please explain when and what part
     of your head was hurt.)

36. Do you hear voices at times,   / YES / NO
     but there isn't anyone around you?

37. Do you have visual hallucinations,   / YES / NO
     where you see things and you are sure
     there is nothing there?

38. Are you sometimes confused about where you are,   / YES / NO
     who you are or what you are doing
     for a period of time?

39. Are there times when you *suddenly*   / YES / NO
     become hysterical?

40. Do you have periods of unexplained nervousness?   / YES / NO

41. Do you have feelings of having been someplace or   / YES / NO
     known someone in the past whom you
     haven't known or had contact with? *(déjà vu)*

42.   Do you have short lapses of memory?   / YES / NO
      (if yes, is it due to alcohol, drugs, other or
      unknown reasons—circle which one)

43.   Have you been told that you have a starring or   / YES / NO
      dazed expression for short periods of time?

44.   Do you all of a sudden get drowsy for   / YES / NO
      a brief period?

45.   Do you have times when you start drooling,   / YES / NO
      muttering or mumbling? *(if yes, circle which one.)*

46.   Are there times when you have difficulty speaking, / YES / NO
      unclear speech or say words that don't make sense?
      (if yes, circle which one.)

47.   Do you suddenly act crazy for no reason and   / YES / NO
      then you are back to your usual self
      a few minutes later?
      (ex. do something totally out of character)

48.   Do you have periods of automatic behavior?   / YES / NO
      (ex. when your behavior is spontaneous without
      thought or from force of habit)

49.   Do you have sudden periods of weakness of   / YES / NO
      your right arm, right leg, left arm, left leg?
      (if yes, circle which one.)

50.   Do you start perspiring for no particular reason?   / YES / NO
      (ex. you are sitting still and watching TV and
      all of a sudden you start to sweat.)

51. Have you ever injured yourself during   / YES / NO
     the times you experienced any of
     the (phenomena) symptoms or conditions that
     you identified above where you answered yes?

B.   As a child did you ever have the following happen:

1.   Have a head injury?   / YES / NO
     (if yes, please explain when and
     what part of your head was hurt.)

2.   Was there any trauma during your birth?   / YES / NO
     (was your mother sick while she was
     pregnant with you or were there any other
     significant problems during the pregnancy or
     during your birth? If yes please explain.

3.   A history of convulsions?   / YES / NO

4.   Convulsions associated with   / YES / NO
     a high temperature (fever)?

5.   Behavior disorder?   / YES / NO

6.   Temper tantrums?   / YES / NO

7.   Sleepwalking?   / YES / NO

**C.   Please give a description below if you have had any episodes, phe-
     nomena or symptoms.**
     (Here are 3 examples: [*Type 1*] having difficulty speaking for a short
     period of time. [*Type 2*] brief period of confusion. [*Type 3*] get a far

away feeling—like being out of contact with your surroundings—
for a few seconds.

	Type 1	Type 2	Type 3
Description of the episode, phenomena or symptoms	_____	_____	_____
Age when it first started	_____	_____	_____
How often it happens	_____	_____	_____

Please list all medications that have been prescribed for these episodes

Name of Medication	Dosage	When did you start & stop the medication	Were Medications helpful or not
_____	_____	_____	_____
_____	_____	_____	_____
_____	_____	_____	_____
_____	_____	_____	_____
_____	_____	_____	_____
_____	_____	_____	_____
_____	_____	_____	_____
_____	_____	_____	_____
_____	_____	_____	_____
_____	_____	_____	_____
_____	_____	_____	_____
_____	_____	_____	_____

**If possible please indicate the duration (length of time)
of each of the questions below.**

PRECIPITATION: Do you know the possible cause or trigger of the episode?
☐ YES ☐ NO ☐ UNKNOWN   DURATION_____

PRODROME: Do you have a warning that something is about to happen?
☐ YES ☐ NO ☐ UNKNOWN   DURATION_____

AURA: Is there a first part of an episode that you recognize—a strange feeling or sensation at the beginning of an episode? [ex. dizziness]
☐ YES ☐ NO ☐ UNKNOWN   DURATION_____

EPISODE: Describe the episode or episodes in detail.

_____

_____

_____

_____

_____

_____

_____

_____

POST-EPISODE: How do you feel after the episode or episodes?

_____

_____

_____

_____

_____

_____

D.   **Is there any relationship between the various types of episodes, phenomena or symptoms?** (For example: First you start having difficulty speaking for a short period of time [Question #46], then a brief period of confusion followed by a far away feeling—like being out of contact with your surroundings—for a few seconds [Question #38], then you get dizzy [Question #20]. *Your "yes" answers guide us and you towards the identification of clusters of symptoms.*)

_____

_____

_____

_____

_____

_____

_____

E.   1-   Do your episodes, phenomena or   / YES / NO
symptoms awaken you at night?
(if yes, please list which ones) _____

2-   Are your episodes, phenomena or   / YES / NO
symptoms brought on by alcoho?

3-   Are your episodes, phenomena or   / YES / NO
symptoms helped by alcohol?

4-   Are your episodes, phenomena or   / YES / NO
symptoms brought on by watching TV,
using a computer or flickering lights?

5-   Are your episodes, phenomena or   / YES / NO
symptoms brought on by gaining weight or
etaining fluid?

6- Are your episodes, phenomena   / YES / NO
   or symptoms brought on by a menstrual period or
   just before you start your period?

7- Are your episodes, phenomena   / YES / NO
   or symptoms brought on by stress or anxiety?

8- Are your episodes, phenomena or   / YES / NO
   symptoms brought on by excess heat?

9- Are your episodes, phenomena or   / YES / NO
   symptoms brought on by fatigue or lack of sleep?

10- Are your episodes, phenomena or   / YES / NO
    symptoms brought on by hunger or
    insufficient food?

11- Are your episodes, phenomena or   / YES / NO
    symptoms brought on or began developing when
    falling asleep or when you are waking up?

12- Are your episodes, phenomena or   / YES / NO
    symptoms associated with a change in
    your personality after the episode?

Appendix C

General History Form

Personal Identification

Name: _____   Regular treating health practitioners:

Home Address: _____   _____

_____   _____

Home Phone: _____   Type of Insurance: _____

Work Phone: _____

Social Security Number: _____   Person responsible for payment: ___

_____   _____

Sex: ___Height: ___Weight: ____   _____

Date of Birth: _____Age: ____   Address: _____

Place of Birth: _____   _____

Race: _____Religion: _____   Home #: _____Work #: _____

Marital Status: _____   SS#: _____

Last Completed Medical Exam: Date of Birth: _____

_____   _____

Last Grade Finished: _____   Is Litigation involved?   / YES / NO

Occupation: _____   Attorney's name: _____
Do you smoke?   / YES / NO   Address: _____
Do you   / YES / NO   _____
wear a seatbelt?   Telephone: _____
Referred by: _____
Reason For Referral? _____   Industrial Accident?   / YES / NO
_____   Name of Carrier? _____
Date the Problem Began: _____   Address: _____
Date of Injury: _____   _____
Present treating doctors or other   Telephone: _____
health practitioners:

_____
_____   Source of History: _____
_____   History recorded by: _____

IF OVER 18—do you have a Durable Power of   / YES   / NO
Attorney for Health Care or a Living Will?

SIGNATURE: _____   **DATE:** _____

Important! Please read the following directions before you begin. Please complete this form in **ink**. Answer all questions to the best of your knowledge. If you don't know the answer to a question, mark "don't know" by the question. When describing your chief complaint (*if any*) please be sure to mention any unusual circumstances or events associated with the onset of the illness; the duration, frequency, severity, and relation to other events (*i.e. is there anything that makes the illness worse? is there anything that brings on an attack of the illness?*)—Write your descriptions in the space provided or on the last page of this form using the corresponding question number. If any question does not apply to you please write in "N/A" by the question.

If there are any questions you don't understand or would like to discuss, please *circle* the question number.

PLEASE ANSWER THE QUESTIONS IN **BOLD PRINT** FIRST. IF YOU HAVE TIME, GO BACK AND ANSWER THE OTHER QUESTIONS.

---

2. **CHIEF COMPLAINT**: (what is bothering you?)

_____

_____

_____

_____

3. **History of present illness**—tests done, current treatment (*how long?*) and results (*see directions above*):

_____

_____

_____

_____

3.1 Past Treatments and results:

_____

_____

_____

_____

3.2 Residential Treatment Center:

_____

_____

_____

_____

3.3 Psychiatric Treatment:

_____
_____
_____
_____
_____
_____

TESTS and EXAMINATIONS:
(please check YES or NO and provide dates and results if known.)

YES	NO		TESTS	DATE	RESULTS
☐	☐	**3.4**	**Blood tests**	_____	_____
☐	☐	3.5	Brain map	_____	_____
☐	☐	**3.6**	**CAT scan of (_____)**	_____	_____
☐	☐	3.7	EEG	_____	_____
☐	☐	3.8	Gallbladder series	_____	_____
☐	☐	3.9	Large bowel (barium enema)	_____	_____
☐	☐	**3.10**	**MRI of (_____)**	_____	_____
☐	☐	3.11	Myeolgram	_____	_____
☐	☐	3.12	Pyelogram (kidney exam)	_____	_____
☐	☐	3.13	Radio Isotope Exam	_____	_____
☐	☐	3.14	Sonogram of (_____)	_____	_____
☐	☐	3.15	Stomach (upper GI series)	_____	_____
☐	☐	3.16	X-Ray of (_____)	_____	_____
☐	☐	3.17	Other X-rays_____	_____	_____
			_____	_____	_____
☐	☐	**3.18**	**Other tests_____**	_____	_____
			_____	_____	_____
			_____	_____	_____

4. SUMMARY. PLEASE GIVE DETAILS ON THE QUESTIONS YOU ANSWER.

YES NO

☐   ☐   **4.1 Does your medical problem interfere with your life?** Describe your average day from the time you get up until you go to bed at night.

_____

_____

_____

_____

☐   ☐   **4.2 Do you have a family history of any illnesses or other medical conditions?** (Please List)

_____

_____

_____

_____

4.3 IS YOUR CURRENT LIFESTYLE SATISFACTORY WITH RESPECT TO:

☐   ☐   **4.4.1   Work and/or school**_____

_____

_____

_____

☐   ☐   **4.4.2   Play / social activities / hobbies/ sports**_____

_____

_____

_____

YES NO

☐   ☐   4.4.3   Prayer, religious belief or other social support systems, friendships_____

_____

_____

_____

☐   ☐   **4.4.4   Too much stress**_____

_____

_____

_____

☐   ☐   **4.5 Do you have any allergies?**_____

_____

_____

_____

☐   ☐   **4.6 Do you sleep OK and awake rested?**_____

_____

_____

_____

☐   ☐   **4.7 Do you exercise adequately?**_____

_____

_____

_____

☐   ☐   **4.8 Is your quality of life satisfactory?**_____

_____

_____

_____

YES NO
☐   ☐   **4.9 Do you have short episodes of changes in your thinking, mood, feelings, or behavior?**

_____

_____

_____

☐   ☐   **4.10 Have you had frequent infections?**_____

_____

_____

_____

4.11 What other health-related or other problems trouble you?

_____

_____

_____

5. BIRTH, GROWTH and EARLY DEVELOPMENT HISTORY

YES NO   Comments
☐   ☐   **5.1 Was your mother sick**   _____
           while she was   _____
           pregnant with you?   _____
☐   ☐   **5.2 Was your birth normal?**   _____
☐   ☐   5.3 Are you a twin?   _____
☐   ☐   **5.4 Are you adopted?**   _____
In sitting crawling, walking, talking or toilet training were you:
☐   ☐   5.5 average   _____
☐   ☐   5.6 slow   _____
☐   ☐   5.7 early   _____

6. NUTRITION

YES	NO		Comments
☐	☐	**6.1 Is your diet healthy?**	_____
☐	☐	6.2 Do you have a good appetite?	_____
☐	☐	**6.3 Has your appetite increased or**	_____
		decreased recently?	_____
		(please explain)	_____
☐	☐	**6.4 Do you eat regularly?**	_____
☐	☐	6.5 Do you have cravings for	_____
		a specific food?	_____

7. ILLNESS (Illnesses—**PLEASE CHECK**—if you or any blood relative have or had. This includes grandparents, parents, aunts, uncles and 1st and 2nd cousins and great aunts and uncles.)

YES	NO			YOU	FAMILY	
☐	☐	7.1	**Aids or HIV+**	☐	☐	_____
☐	☐	7.2	**Anemia**	☐	☐	_____
☐	☐	7.3	**Allergies, asthma**	☐	☐	_____
☐	☐	7.4	**Alcoholism**	☐	☐	_____
☐	☐	7.5	**Arthritis**	☐	☐	_____
☐	☐	7.6	**Bleeding or**	☐	☐	_____
			clotting problems			_____
☐	☐	7.7	**Cancer or Tumor**	☐	☐	_____
☐	☐	7.8	**Chemical or**	☐	☐	_____
			toxic exposure			_____
☐	☐	7.9	**Chronic Fatigue**	☐	☐	_____
			Syndrome			_____
☐	☐	7.10	**Depression or**	☐	☐	_____
			Nervous breakdown			_____
☐	☐	7.11	**Diabetes**	☐	☐	_____

☐ ☐ 7.12 Drug abuse ☐ ☐ _____

☐ ☐ 7.13 Epilepsy, ☐ ☐ _____
seizures, faints _____

☐ ☐ 7.14 Heart problems ☐ ☐ _____

☐ ☐ 7.15 High blood pressure ☐ ☐ _____

☐ ☐ 7.16 Low blood pressure ☐ ☐ _____

☐ ☐ 7.17 Headaches, migraine ☐ ☐ _____

☐ ☐ 7.18 Infections—recurrent ☐ ☐ _____

☐ ☐ 7.19 Tuberculosis ☐ ☐ _____

☐ ☐ 7.20 Stomach problems ☐ ☐ _____
or ulcers _____

☐ ☐ 7.21 Thyroid disease ☐ ☐ _____

☐ ☐ 7.22 Moodiness ☐ ☐ _____

☐ ☐ 7.23 Clean freak ☐ ☐ _____

☐ ☐ 7.24 Hoard—can't ☐ ☐ _____
throw things out _____

☐ ☐ 7.25 Other illness ☐ ☐ _____

8. IMMUNIZATIONS and TESTS

YES NO

☐ ☐ 8.1 Have you received _____
all your childhood immunizations? _____

☐ ☐ 8.2 Have you had a tetanus shot in _____
the last 5 years? _____

☐ ☐ 8.3 Have you had any _____
recent blood tests? _____

☐ ☐ **8.4 Have you had any
immunizations that you were** _____
allergic or sensitive to? (*if yes: which ones?*)

9. HOSPITALIZATIONS and ACCIDENTS

YES NO

☐   ☐   **9.1   Have you had any operations
in the past year?**
(*If yes: what and when?*)   _____
                                              _____
                                              _____

☐   ☐   9.2   Have you ever had and
operation/surgery?
(If yes: what and when?)   _____
                                              _____
                                              _____

☐   ☐   **9.3   Have you had any
serious accidents in thepast year?**
(*If yes: what and when?*)   _____
                                              _____
                                              _____

☐   ☐   **9.4   Have you ever had any
head injuries** (*If yes: what area of
your head and when?*)   _____
                                              _____
                                              _____

☐   ☐   9.4   Have you ever had a
serious accident?
(*If yes: what and when?*)   _____
                                              _____
                                              _____

10. MEDICATIONS.

Any allergic   **10.1 Please list the medications
reaction?   you are presently taking regularly.**
Does it help?
YES NO   Medication   Dates of use
☐   ☐   _____   ☐   ☐
☐   ☐   _____   ☐   ☐
☐   ☐   _____   ☐   ☐

☐ ☐ _____ ☐ ☐
☐ ☐ _____ ☐ ☐
☐ ☐ _____ ☐ ☐
☐ ☐ _____ ☐ ☐
☐ ☐ _____ ☐ ☐
☐ ☐ _____ ☐ ☐
☐ ☐ _____ ☐ ☐

Any allergic   **10.2 Please list the medications you have taken**
reaction?   **in the past.**
Does it help?

YES NO   Medication   Dates of use
☐   ☐   _____   ☐ ☐
☐   ☐   _____   ☐ ☐
☐   ☐   _____   ☐ ☐
☐   ☐   _____   ☐ ☐
☐   ☐   _____   ☐ ☐
☐   ☐   _____   ☐ ☐
☐   ☐   _____   ☐ ☐
☐   ☐   _____   ☐ ☐

YES NO **11. ALLERGIES**   **Comments**
☐   ☐   11.1 Are you allergic to   _____
               certain foods?   _____
☐   ☐   11.2 Are you allergic or   _____
               sensitive to plants?   _____
☐   ☐   11.3 Are you allergic to   _____
               inhalants?   _____
☐   ☐   11.4 Are you allergic to solvents?_____
               (*e.g. gasoline fumes,*   _____
               perfume, paint,   _____
               cleaning agents, etc…)   _____

☐   ☐   11.5 Do you have a
history of hives?   _____

_____

12. FAMILY HISTORY
12.1 **Refer to item number 7 as a guide regarding illnesses they have.**

	Age (if living)	Present health G = Good F = Fair P = Poor	Age at death (if deceased)
Father			
Mother			
Brother 1			
Sister 2			
3			
4			
5			
6			

YES NO

☐   ☐   **12.2 Do you have children?**   _____
If yes, how many?   _____

☐   ☐   **12.3 Have any relatives taken**   _____
medications that have   _____
helped them with   _____
problems similar to yours?   _____
If yes, please describe: _____
(Include other distant blood relatives also.)

YES NO **12.4 Marital status:**
☐   ☐   **single**
☐   ☐   **married**
☐   ☐   **widowed**

12.5 For how many years?   _____

12.6 Number of marriages: _____

YES NO 13.PERSONAL HISTORY

☐ ☐ 13.1 Are you shy?

☐ ☐ 13.2 Are you easy to get along with?

☐ ☐ 13.3 Do you have good personal hygiene?

☐ ☐ 13.4 Do you sleep enough, and feel rested in the morning?

☐ ☐ 13.5 Average hours of sleep (circle one)
            4 5 6 7 8 9, or_____

☐ ☐ 13.6 Are you right-handed?

☐ ☐ 13.7 Have you been on any   _____
            special diet in the past year?_____
            If yes, what kind?   _____

☐ ☐ 13.8 Highest weight: _____Year: _____

☐ ☐ 13.9 Lowest weight: _____Year: _____

☐ ☐ 13.10 Are you physically challenged in any way?

☐ ☐ 13.11 Do you have any body deformities?

☐ ☐ **13.12 Do you have decreased energy?**

☐ ☐ 13.13 Do you have many aches and pains throughout yourbody?

YES NO 14.SOCIAL HISTORY

☐ ☐ 14.1 Do you get along with your siblings?

☐ ☐ 14.2 Do you get along with your peers?

☐ ☐ 14.3 Do you have a good relationship with your parents?

☐ ☐ 14.4 Are your weekend activities interesting or boring?

☐ ☐ 14.5 Do others live in   _____
            your home? Who?   _____

☐   ☐   14.6 For children—15 and younger—Who are you with after school and at night? (*Please Describe*)

_____

_____

YES NO **15.HABITS**

☐   ☐   15.1 Do you have any hobbies?
☐   ☐   15.2 Are you generally happy with your life?
☐   ☐   15.3 Do you have cravings for _____
          a specific food? Which one?_____
☐   ☐   **15.4 Are you a perfectionist?**
☐   ☐   15.5 Are you obsessive or compulsive?

Has there been a history of:
☐   ☐   15.6 Head banging?
☐   ☐   15.7 Bedwetting?
☐   ☐   15.8 Nail biting?
☐   ☐   15.9 Nightmares?
☐   ☐   15.10 Speech problems?

☐   ☐   **15.11 Are there discipline problems?**
☐   ☐   15.12 Are there problems between parents?
☐   ☐   15.13 Do you get upset if things aren't exactly as they should be?
☐   ☐   15.14 Do you have regular bowel movements?
☐   ☐   15.15 Do you have satisfactory sex?
☐   ☐   15.16 Do you watch television? _____
          How many hours per day? _____
☐   ☐   15.17 Do you read? _____
          How many hours per day? _____
☐   ☐   15.18 Do you have regular vacations?
☐   ☐   15.19 Do you travel much?

Do you use:	Never	Occasionally	Often	Daily
☐ ☐ 15.16 Laxatives	☐	☐	☐	☐
☐ ☐ 15.17 Vitamins	☐	☐	☐	☐
☐ ☐ **15.18 Sedatives**	☐	☐	☐	☐
☐ ☐ 15.19 Diet Pills	☐	☐	☐	☐
☐ ☐ 15.20 Cold Pills	☐	☐	☐	☐
☐ ☐ 15.21 Coffee	☐	☐	☐	☐

Number of cups per day:_____

☐ ☐ **15.22 Alcohol**	☐	☐	☐	☐
☐ ☐ 15.23 Cigars/pipe	☐	☐	☐	☐
☐ ☐ 15.24 Chewing tobacco	☐	☐	☐	☐
☐ ☐ 15.25 Herb remedies	☐	☐	☐	☐
☐ ☐ 15.26 Other remedies not requiring prescription	☐	☐	☐	☐
☐ ☐ 15.27 Cigarettes	☐	☐	☐	☐

Number of packs / day: _____, for _____years.

☐ ☐ 15.28 Have you increased or decreased any of the above items since your present illness or accident?
If yes, which one(s): _____

☐ ☐ 15.29 Have you ever been treated for alcoholism or drug abuse?

☐ ☐ 15.30 Do you use street drugs?

16.SCHOOL HISTORY—(If you are attending school now—describe generally—how is it going at school and if there are any problems)

_____

_____

16.1 **Highest grade completed:** _____

16.2 Years of business or technical school: _____

16.3 Years of college: _____

16.4 Field of study: _____

16.5 Degrees obtained: _____

YES NO

☐ ☐ **16.6 Do you have** _____
problems reading? _____

☐ ☐ **16.7 Do you have** _____
problems writing? _____

☐ ☐ **16.8 Do you have** _____
problems with math? _____

17.WORK HISTORY

YES NO   **Comments**

☐ ☐ **17.1 Do you have a job?** _____
(full-time or part-time) _____

☐ ☐ **17.2 Describe your present job and** _____
length of time there. _____

☐ ☐ 17.3 Describe your previous job, _____
length of time there and _____
reason for leaving. _____

☐ ☐ 17.4 Is your present job improving _____
or changing? _____

☐ ☐ 17.5 Is your income improving _____
or changing? _____

☐ ☐ **17.6 Do you like your job** _____
(or school)? _____

☐ ☐ 17.7 Are your average _____
work activities interesting? _____

18. REVIEW of SYSTEMS

YES NO

☐ ☐ **18.1   Skin.**
☐ ☐ **18.1.1 skin color changes**   _____
☐ ☐ 18.1.2 nail changes   _____
☐ ☐ 18.1.3 hair changes   _____
☐ ☐ 18.1.4 itching   _____
☐ ☐ 18.1.5 growths   _____
☐ ☐ 18.1.6 birth marks   _____
☐ ☐ 18.1.7 rashes   _____

☐ ☐ **18.2   Hematologic**   _____
☐ ☐ **18.2.1 Do you have**   _____
         frequent swollen glands?   _____
☐ ☐ 18.2.2 Have you ever had   _____
         a blood transfusion?   _____
☐ ☐ 18.2.3 Do you donate blood   _____
         regularly? How often?   _____

    18.3   **Central Nervous System**
Do you have frequent or severe problems with:
☐ ☐ **18.3.1   Headaches**   _____
☐ ☐ **18.3.2   Seizures**   _____
☐ ☐ 18.3.3   Blindness   _____
☐ ☐ 18.3.4   Paralysis   _____
☐ ☐ 18.3.5   Muscle weakness   _____
☐ ☐ **18.3.6   Unsteadiness**   _____
☐ ☐ 18.3.7   Tingling   _____
☐ ☐ **18.3.8   Confusion**   _____
☐ ☐ **18.3.9   Fainting**   _____
☐ ☐ 18.3.10 Weakness   _____

YES	NO		Comments
☐	☐	18.3.11 Shaking	_____
☐	☐	18.3.12 Numbness	_____
☐	☐	**18.3.13 Dizziness**	_____
☐	☐	18.3.14 Double vision	_____
☐	☐	18.3.15 Change in handwriting	_____
☐	☐	**18.3.16 Slow, progressive memory impairment**	_____
☐	☐	18.3.17 Episodes of sudden strange smells or taste	_____
☐	☐	**18.3.18 Frequent changes in behavior (e.g. mood swings)**	_____
☐	☐	18.3.19 Do you ever have trouble doing something you've already learned how to do?	_____
☐	☐	18.3.20 Problem with fine finger movements?	_____
☐	☐	18.3.21 Are you clumsy?	_____

		18.4	**Eyes**	**Comments**
YES	NO	Do you wear		
☐	☐	18.4.1	glasses?	_____
☐	☐	18.4.2	contacts?	_____
☐	☐	18.4.3	Do you have blind spots?	_____
☐	☐	18.4.4	Do you have large amounts of tearing?	_____
☐	☐	**18.4.5**	**Have you ever had other problems with your eyes?**	_____
☐	☐	18.4.6	Date of last eye exam?	_____

YES	NO	**18.5**	**Ear, nose, throat and mouth**	
☐	☐	**18.5.1**	**loss of hearing**	_____
☐	☐	18.5.2	buzzing or ringing in ears	_____

☐ ☐ 18.5.3 ear drainage _____
☐ ☐ 18.5.4 earaches _____
☐ ☐ **18.5.5 sinusitis** _____
☐ ☐ 18.5.6 nosebleeds _____
☐ ☐ **18.5.7 constant stuffy/runny nose**_____
☐ ☐ 18.5.8 hoarseness _____
☐ ☐ 18.5.9 pain about nose or eyes _____
☐ ☐ **18.5.10 enlarged thyroid** _____
☐ ☐ 18.5.11 enlargements in neck _____
☐ ☐ 18.5.12 false teeth _____
☐ ☐ 18.5.13 swollen gums _____
☐ ☐ 18.5.14 unfilled teeth cavities _____
☐ ☐ 18.5.15 dental work in past year _____
☐ ☐ 18.5.16 sore tongue _____
☐ ☐ 18.5.17 change in taste sensation _____
☐ ☐ 18.5.18 change in smelling sensation_____

YES NO 18.6 **Respiratory** _____
☐ ☐ **18.6.1 shortness of breath** _____
☐ ☐ **18.6.2 cough up blood or sputum**_____
☐ ☐ **18.6.3 wheezing** _____
☐ ☐ 18.6.4 coughing spells _____
☐ ☐ 18.6.5 emphysema _____
☐ ☐ **18.6.6 frequent colds** _____

YES NO 18.7 Cardiovascular
☐ ☐ **18.7.1 chest pains when excited,** _____
        upset, or when you _____
        exert yourself _____
☐ ☐ 18.7.2 heart murmur _____
☐ ☐ 18.7.3 chest pain which _____
        radiates down arm _____

☐ ☐ **18.7.4 high blood pressure** _____

☐ ☐ 18.7.5 shortness of breath at night _____

☐ ☐ 18.7.6 leg cramps _____

☐ ☐ 18.7.7 racing heart at times _____

☐ ☐ 18.7.8 pain in legs when walking _____

☐ ☐ 18.7.9 varicose veins _____

☐ ☐ **18.7.10 swollen feet or ankles** _____

☐ ☐ 18.7.11 fingers or toes become
white, cold _____

YES NO 18.8 **Gastrointestinal**

☐ ☐ 18.8.1 difficulty swallowing _____

☐ ☐ 18.8.2 gas _____

☐ ☐ **18.8.3 recent changes in
bowel habits** _____

☐ ☐ 18.8.4 nausea _____

☐ ☐ **18.8.5 abdominal pain** _____

☐ ☐ **18.8.6 constipation** _____

☐ ☐ 18.8.7 rectal bleeding _____

☐ ☐ 18.8.8 indigestion _____

☐ ☐ 18.8.9 vomiting blood _____

☐ ☐ **18.8.10 diarrhea** _____

☐ ☐ 18.8.11 gray stools _____

☐ ☐ 18.8.12 vomiting _____

☐ ☐ 18.8.13 rectal pain _____

☐ ☐ 18.8.14 black or bloody stools _____

☐ ☐ 18.8.15 inability to eat certain
foods (which ones?) _____

☐ ☐ 18.8.16 hemorrhoids _____

☐ ☐ **18.8.17 history of ulcers** _____

YES NO 18.9 **Urinary**

☐   ☐   18.9.1 pain on urination _____

☐   ☐   **18.9.2 blood in urine** _____

☐   ☐   18.9.3 difficulty starting urination _____

☐   ☐   18.9.4 urinary infections _____

☐   ☐   18.9.5 wet pants or bed _____

☐   ☐   18.9.6 urinary or kidney stones _____

18.9.7 get up at night to _____
urinate (how many times?) _____

YES NO 18.10 **Male genital system**

☐   ☐   **18.10.1 pain or soreness about** _____
the penis or testicles _____

☐   ☐   **18.10.2 loss or impairment** _____
of sexual function _____

☐   ☐   18.10.3 unusual discharge _____

☐   ☐   18.10.4 prostate trouble _____

☐   ☐   18.10.5 concerned about _____
masturbation

YES NO 18.11 **Female genital system**

☐   ☐   **18.11.1 menstrual problems** _____

☐   ☐   18.11.2 premenstrual problems _____

☐   ☐   18.11.3 bleeding between periods _____

☐   ☐   18.11.4 unusual vaginal discharge _____

☐   ☐   18.11.5 lumps in breasts _____

☐   ☐   **18.11.6 Have you had any** _____
pregnancies?Number: _____

☐   ☐   **18.11.7 Are you menstruating** _____
now? Age of onset: _____

☐   ☐   **18.11.8 Are you menopausal?** _____
Age of onset: _____

☐   ☐   **18.11.9**   **Are you taking** _____
                       birth control pills? _____
☐   ☐   18.11.10 concerned about _____
                      masturbation

YES NO   18.12 **Musculoskeletal system**
☐   ☐   **18.12.1 aches or stiffness in joints** _____
☐   ☐   **18.12.2 weakness in arms or legs** _____
☐   ☐   18.12.3 aching neck _____
☐   ☐   18.12.4 aching shoulders or back _____
☐   ☐   18.12.5 decreased muscle size _____
☐   ☐   18.12.6 night cramps _____
☐   ☐   18.12.7 tire easily _____

YES NO   18.13 **Endocrine system**
☐   ☐   18.13.1   unusually sensitive to _____
                      heat or cold _____
☐   ☐   **18.13.2   excessive thirst** _____
☐   ☐   18.13.3   excessive hunger _____
☐   ☐   18.13.4   excessive urination _____
☐   ☐   18.13.5   excessive perspiration _____
☐   ☐   **18.13.6   hair changes** _____
        18.13.7   changes in libido _____
                      (sex drive) _____
☐   ☐   18.13.8   fluid retention _____
                      (swelling of legs) _____
☐   ☐   **18.13.9   treated in the past** _____
                      with thyroid or _____
                      other hormones _____
☐   ☐   18.13.10 disturbances in growth _____

YES NO   18.14 **Psychological**

☐   ☐   18.14.1   nervous around strangers _____

☐   ☐   **18.14.2   bad temper** _____

☐   ☐   **18.14.3   frequent crying** _____

☐   ☐   **18.14.4   difficulty**
                    making decisions _____

☐   ☐   **18.14.5   suicidal impulses** _____

☐   ☐   **18.14.6   extreme happy or**
                    sad periods _____

☐   ☐   18.14.7   marked decrease in energy_____

☐   ☐   18.14.8   depression _____

☐   ☐   18.14.9   problems with
                    attention or concentration_____

☐   ☐   18.14.10 problems with anxiety _____

☐   ☐   **18.14.11 periods of feeling**
                    paranoid or suspicious _____

☐   ☐   18.14.12 Has anyone ever told you _____
                    that you have a _____
                    behavior problem? _____

YES NO   18.15 **Autonomic nervous system**

☐   ☐   When you get excited, do you…

☐   ☐   18.15.1 breathe fast _____

☐   ☐   18.15.2 get nauseated _____

☐   ☐   18.15.3 get headaches _____

☐   ☐   18.15.4 get a dry mouth _____

☐   ☐   **18.15.5 get diarrhea** _____

☐   ☐   18.15.6 get unusually warm or
                  cold fingers or toes _____

YES NO 18.16 **Stress**

☐ ☐ **18.16.1 Under pressure,** _____
do you become ill? _____
If yes, what symptoms _____
do you get? _____

YES NO 19. **Environmental History**

At work or at home, are you frequently exposed to...

☐ ☐ **19.1 chemicals** _____
☐ ☐ 19.2 solvents _____
☐ ☐ 19.3 cleaning fluids _____
☐ ☐ 19.4 gas _____
☐ ☐ **19.5 loud noises** _____
☐ ☐ 19.6 gas fumes _____
☐ ☐ **19.7 insect sprays** _____
☐ ☐ 19.8 motor fumes _____
☐ ☐ 19.9 neighborhood problems _____
☐ ☐ **19.10 Do your friends, family,** _____
co-workers have any _____
medical problems that _____
may be related to your _____
medical problems? _____
(ex. smog exposure, flu, TB, AIDS)
If yes, describe briefly:

20.**Effect of health problem. Please describe how your health problem (illness, accident or other) has affected your:**

Diet: _____

_____

_____

_____

Exercise: _____

_____

_____

_____

Life style (schedule, work, play, other activities): _____

_____

_____

_____

21. What do you think can be done to help you?

_____

_____

_____

A Final Note

What's Important
An Overview of Timing, Continuity and Follow-up Interventions

For our purposes, an intervention is any action (or in some cases omission of an option) that should be considered in dealing with a problem. This includes the questions that may be posed by a family member or teacher about a child of pre-school or school age. For example, suppose a student seems to get into fights too often, or says she is afraid, or won't listen to anyone. He or she should be referred to the school nurse or a special education teacher for an opinion. Also, if some educational or medical or school or home schedule change is considered—whether it is acted upon or not—this is a relevant intervention.

It is very important to act early, but not too early. The critical matter is that of the proper timing of an intervention. Often, a combination of interventions, involving matters such as class placement, parental counseling, laboratory tests, and medical treatments are needed. They may determine whether a child is treated successfully or not. Many times an intervention is harmful or helpful—based on when it is done, whether is continuity in the treatment and collaboration with others involved (both at home and school) and what followup and corrective feedback takes place.

New ideas, tests and treatments

There have been and will continue to be many new ideas, tests and treatments being developed that deal with what to do and when to do it. Many of these "new" treatments are really refinements of "old" or rediscovered treatments. Some, of course, are really new and useful.

It is critical to realize that new does not mean better or appropriate for this child at this time. This becomes an important decision to work out with the child, family and treatment team in a timely manner.

New diagnostic screens for different learning difficulties are available. Also, new blood tests and metabolic studies have been developed. There are also new techniques for electroencephalographic (EEG) studies, magnetic resonance imaging (MRI), positron emission tomography (PET) scans, and immunological studies.

Identification of PANDAS (Pediatric Autoimmune Neuropsychiatric Disorders Associated with streptococcal infections) is sometimes associated with an obssesive compulsive disorder that responds to intravenous gamma globulin or plamapheresis.

Also many new medications are useful: Adderall, Topomax, Lamictal, Zyprexa, Gabatril, Effexor and many others.

Biofeedback, video-game therapy, distance learning with video conferencing and e-mail home-work assistance, recreational/ sports therapy and many other techniques are useful.

Support groups have great value.

Finally, with the assistance of an unbiased,,competent specialist, review the totality of what is and was done in what combination.

Continue to try and have HOPE. Sometimes the hope can be lead to greater success with a fresh look and approach.